Humanitarian Contributions
Racial Reconciliation

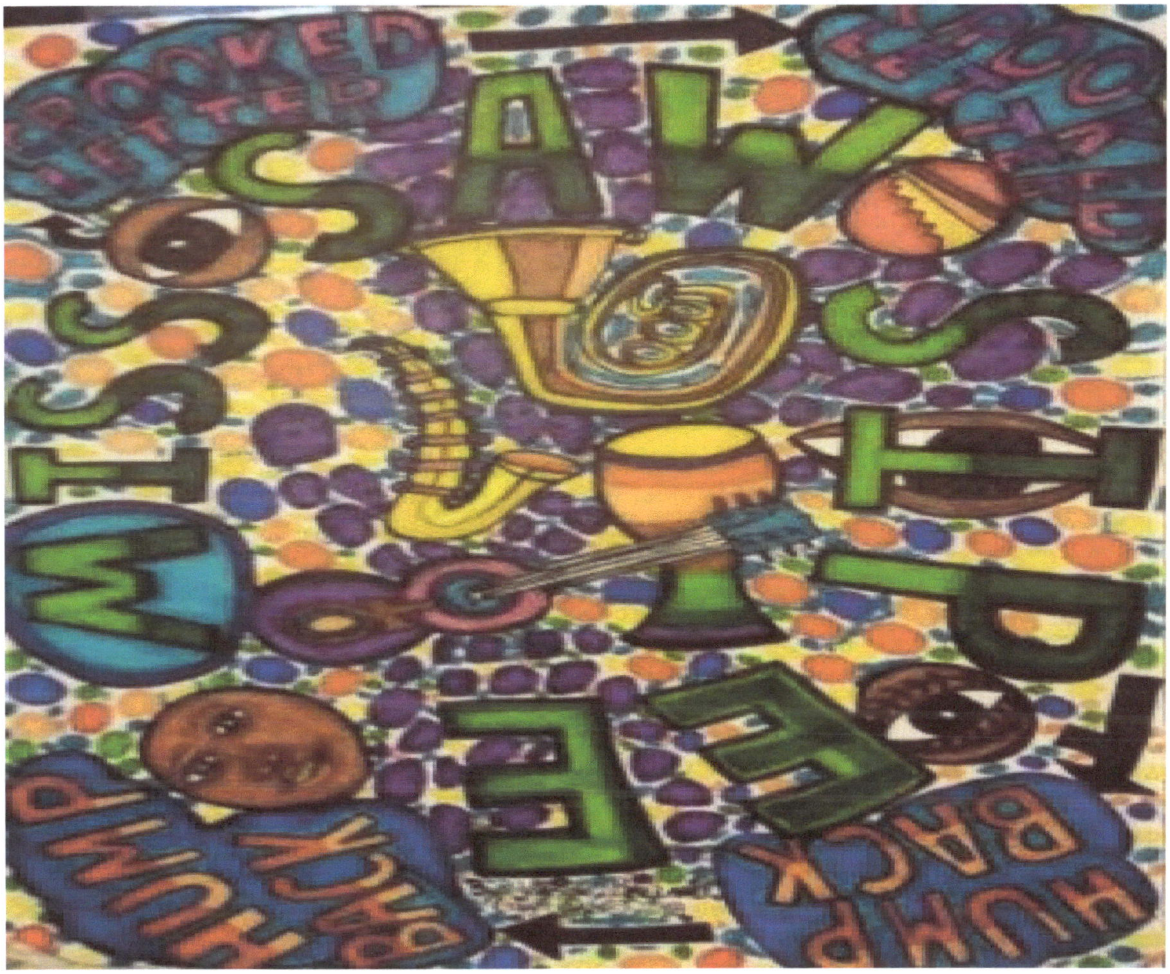

By Min. Vinson Ballard, M.S.

Copyrights © 2018   By Vinson Ballard
ISBN - 10 1729717381
ISBN – 13 9781729717387
Published By Creative Space
No part of this publication may be reproduced or transmitted in any form or by any means, electronically or mechanically including photocopying, recording or any information storage and retrieval system without permission from author, Vinson Ballard.

Tables of Content

Introduction		pp. 4-9
Chapter 1	**Contributions**	pp. 6-20
Chapter 2	**Humanitarian 101**	pp. 21-30
Chapter 3	**Family Dynamics**	pp. 31-43
Chapter 4	**Reconciliation**	pp. 44-60
Chapter 5	**Putting Together**	pp. 61 – 73
Conclusion		pp. 74 – pp. 76

Introduction

This publication is a humble attempt to offer the reader or willing participant assistance with dealing with the issue of humanitarian contributions and the notion of racial reconciliation. It has been shown that the issue of humanitarian contributions varies depending on whose twist is put into it being brought to the surface for consideration. Likewise, the issue of racial reconciliation may also be dealt with in the same fashion.

This publication further will showcase these topics of humanitarian contributions and racial reconciliation through the original creative art by author and professional humanitarian Minister Vinson Ballard. From a wide range of his humbling skillset, this publication will be brought forward in that manner. From a five chapter format, this original creative art will be made available to the reader and willing participant. Additionally, each chapter will also bring forth relative original art pieces towards the thought of Humanitarian Contributions and Racial Reconciliation.

To further illustrate this point of focus the chapters individually will relate the following summary thoughts: 1) Chapter one, Contributions; 2) Chapter Two, Humanitarian 101; 3) Chapter Three,

Family Dynamics; 4) Chapter Four, Reconciliation; 5) Chapter Five, Putting It Together. Altogether, these original art pieces and their relative information brings out of the box information not typical brought forward to the reader or willing participant.

Chapter One (1)

Contributions

Contributions refer to the favorable acts that an individual or individuals made that in some way helped to maintain and/or bring about progress in some manner. It could further be thought of as bringing about an asset versus being a menace that takes away in a negative point of view. Contributions also speak to how an individual or individuals participates in their life's mission towards leaving their legacy favorably in all sincerity. Therefore, the original listing of art pieces in chapter one will delve into this out of the box perspective regarding the joint issue of humanitarian contributions and racial reconciliation.

Chapter One Original Art Listings

1. Healing Warrior
2. Consciousness
3. Good Behavior
4. Smile
5. Who Will

Original Art/ Healing Warrior

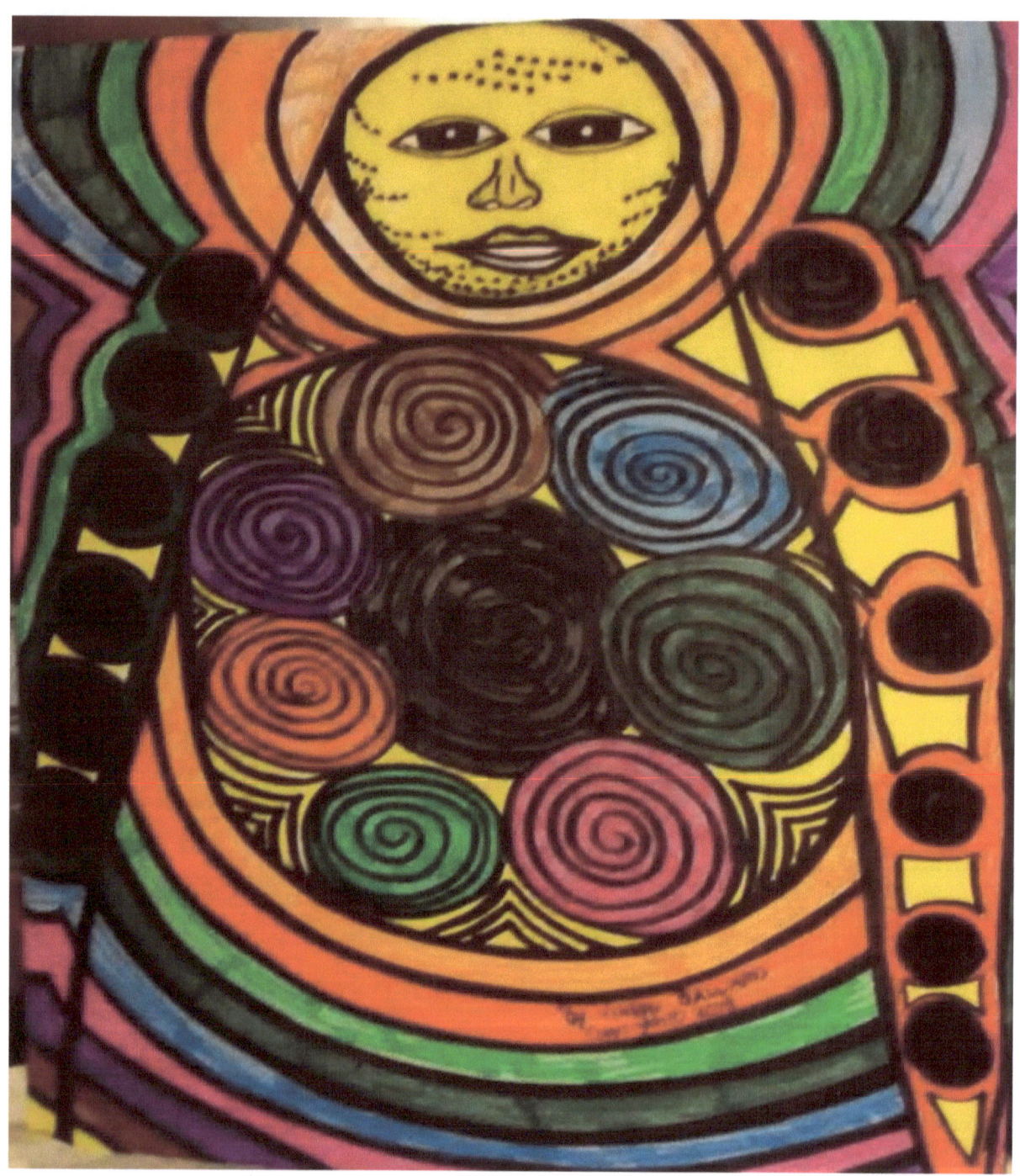

Original Strategy
(Healing Warrior)

This original piece of art takes a very different view of the source typically known as the Sun. It views the Sun as a healing warrior to the greatest extinct imaged. This comes based on the information from entities like NASA that claim the Sun to be a middle aged star. It further takes into account of the Sun being approximately millions of miles and years away that further demonstrates its remarkable ability to impact our galaxy.

Therefore, the original depiction of the Sun in this original piece of art is noted to be profoundly real. The black dots in its face reflect the very constant presence of Melanin, kem or black dot in its existence. The colorful spiral shapes and relative scenery indicate the ever presence of energy engaged in the Sun's very impacting pathway that benefits so many and so much.

Another primary source that speaks to the Cosmos, the Sun and the dynamics that are connected with it is called the Shabaka Stone. An ancient group of individuals from Mali West Africa are known as being the star watchers. They have remarkable contributions to society that express these sentiments.

Equally so is to also mention the impact that the Sun has on all life on Earth, the vegetation, the air and it's amazing but magical energy from its sunlight. From that particular standpoint, the healing warrior reference seems very fitting.

Original Art
(Consciousness)

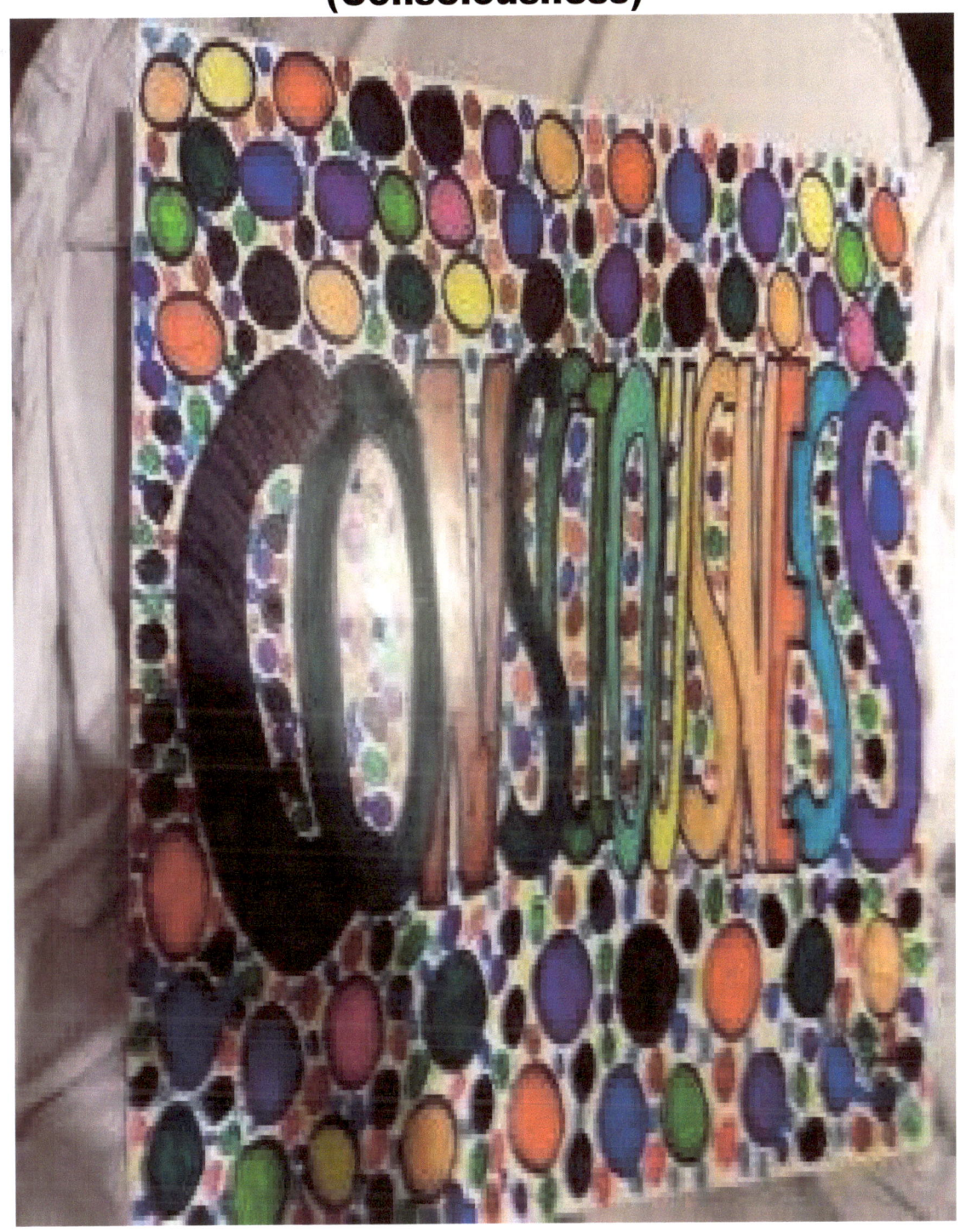

Original Strategy

This is an original view of consciousness as energy that propels everything. It is not limited to anything or anybody and therefore is energy that propels everything. It also is fitting to say that this speaks to the higher priority importance of how all is connected to universality. Of course, this universality also speaks to the dire importance of how everything and everybody is into a momentum of oneness as this art identifies.

Original Art
(Good Behavior)

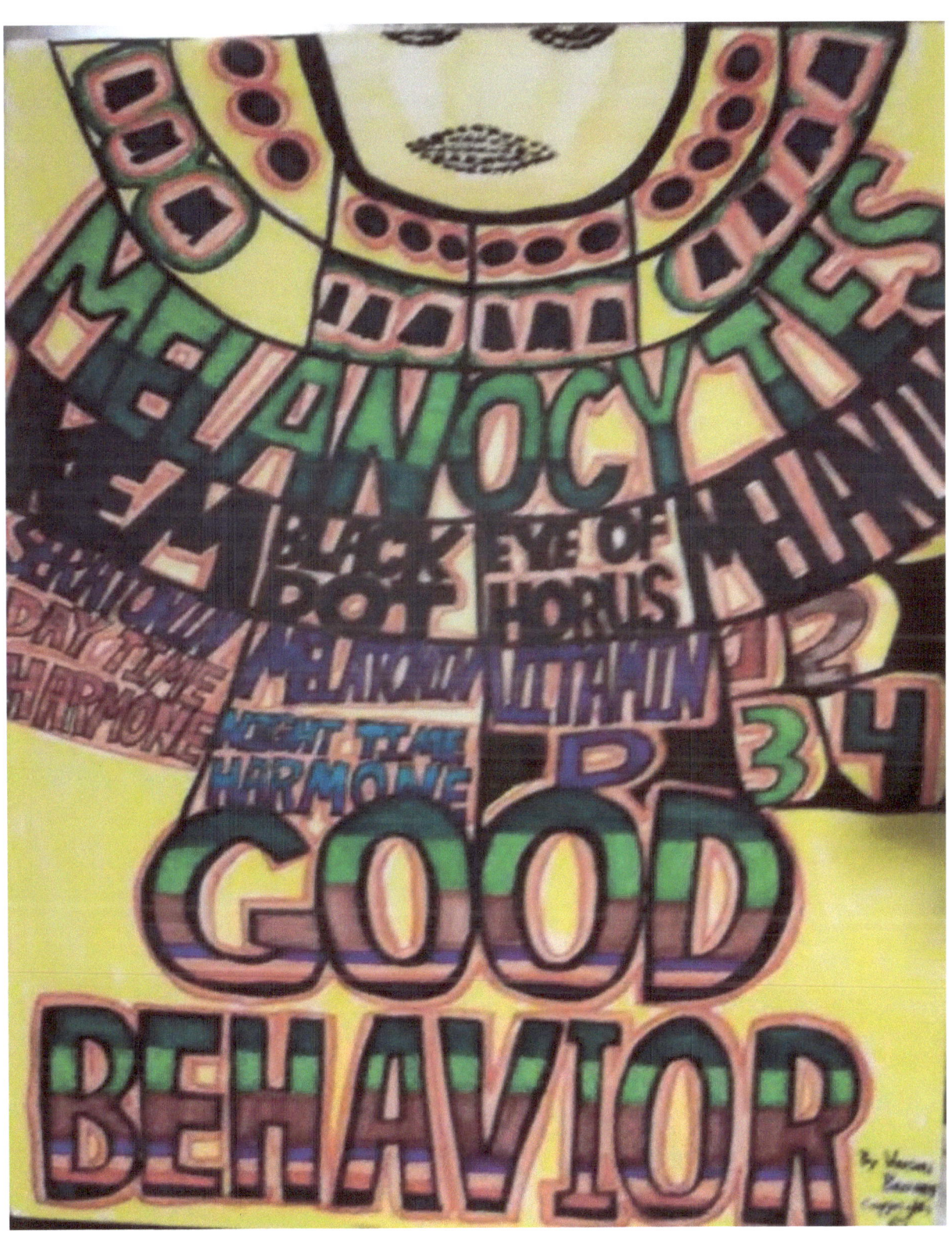

Original Strategy

This speaks to the biological importance of the concept of Good Behavior and its association with Kem, Black Dot and its relevance to the Melanocytes which produces it (Kem, Black Dot and Melanin). Some references that may be viewed separately from this original publication that may have supporting documentation may be found through the works of experts like Dr. Richard King's work <u>Melanin: Keys to Freedom</u> and his exceptional further work on *Black Dot*.

Equally so culturally is the reference to good behavior from the concept of Kemetology, ancient Kemet and the classical African language of Medu Netcher which is important to this particular point of reference.

Original Art
(Smile)

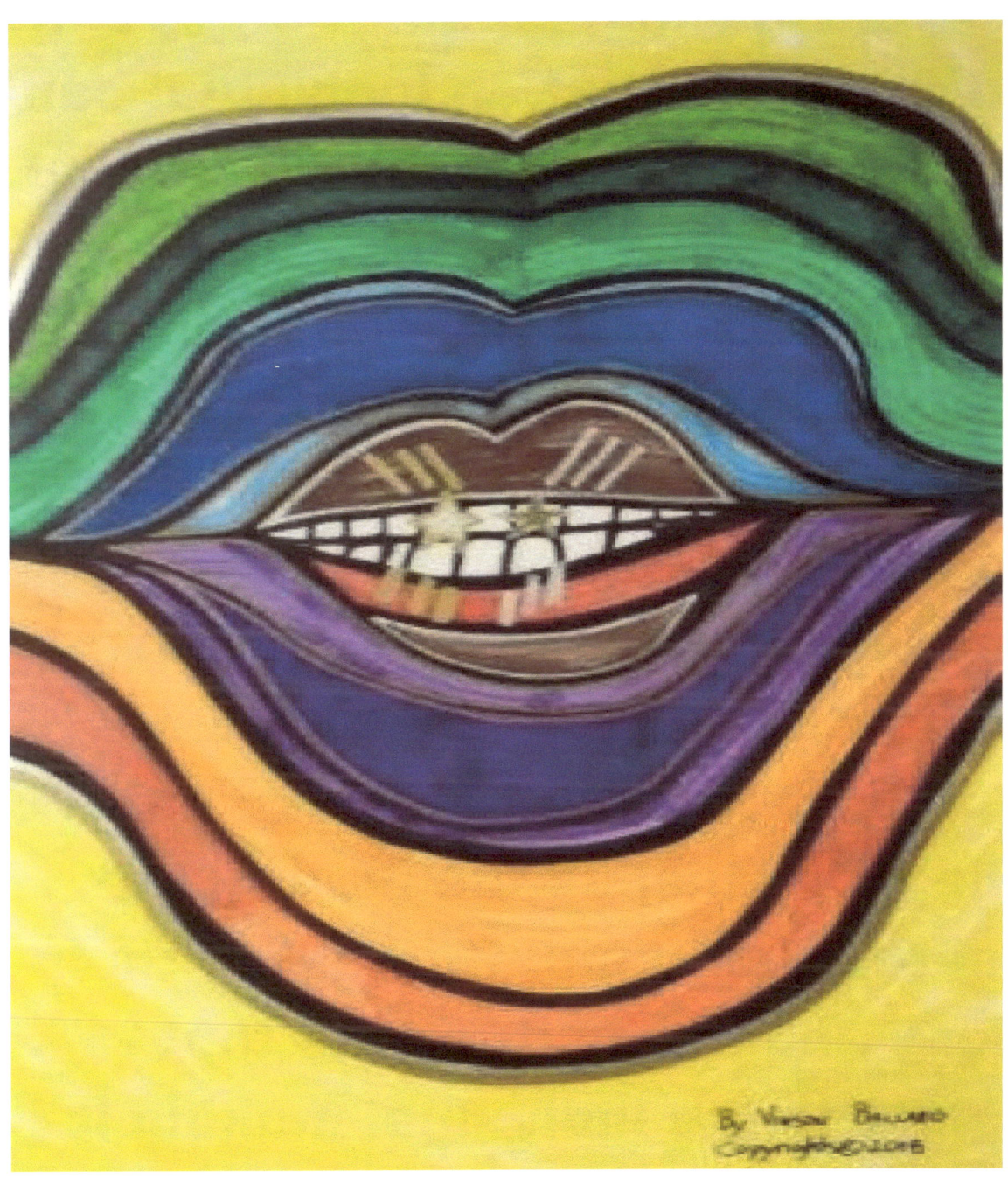

Original Strategy

This original piece of art speaks to the smile that an individual can give within their facial expression. The smile gives a sense that the individual giving the smile is doing OK at that particular instance. Furthermore, the smile can also indicate the other part of the individual is surviving. From a collective perspective, it could speak to the wellbeing like parts of the individual as the mouth, the teeth, their head, the rest of their body and even situations that relate to the individual making it through another day.

Original Art
(Honor... the Love Seat)

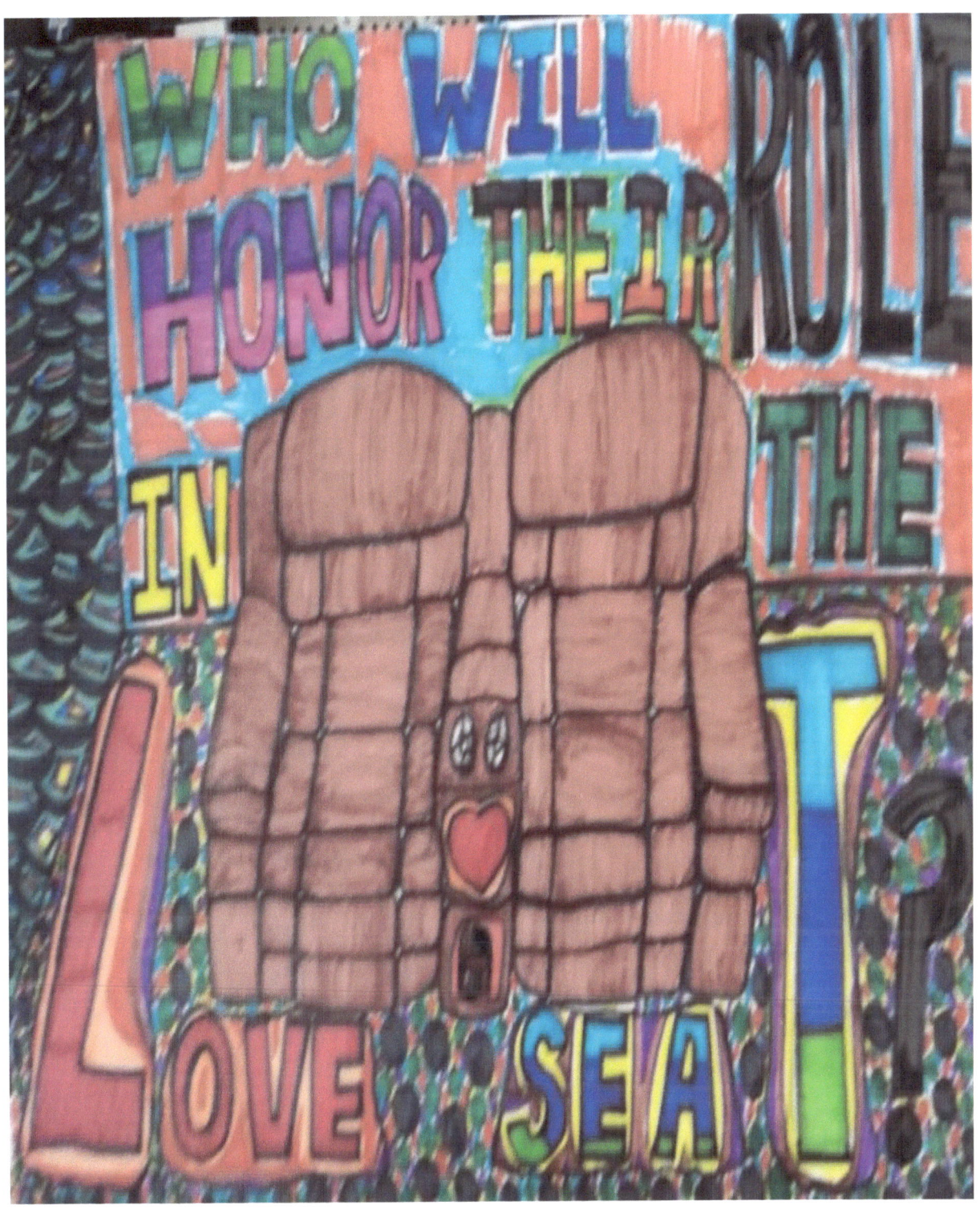

Original Strategy

This speaks to the divine responsibility and opportunity of parents and adults actively working in harmony in as a higher priority manner possible complementary to their life's journey.

Chapter Two (2)

Humanitarian 101

The focus on the related contributing issue of Humanitarian 101 in chapter two refers to the basics or fundamental soundness that is connected to the commitment, decency and genuine care that is connected to this particular reality. Humanitarian refers to an individual being humane and the very higher prioritized association with being as wise and basic as possible during these actions. Chapter two brings a listing of original art pieces that makes this plight for this beneficial kind of out of the box information.

Original Art
(Black Folks)

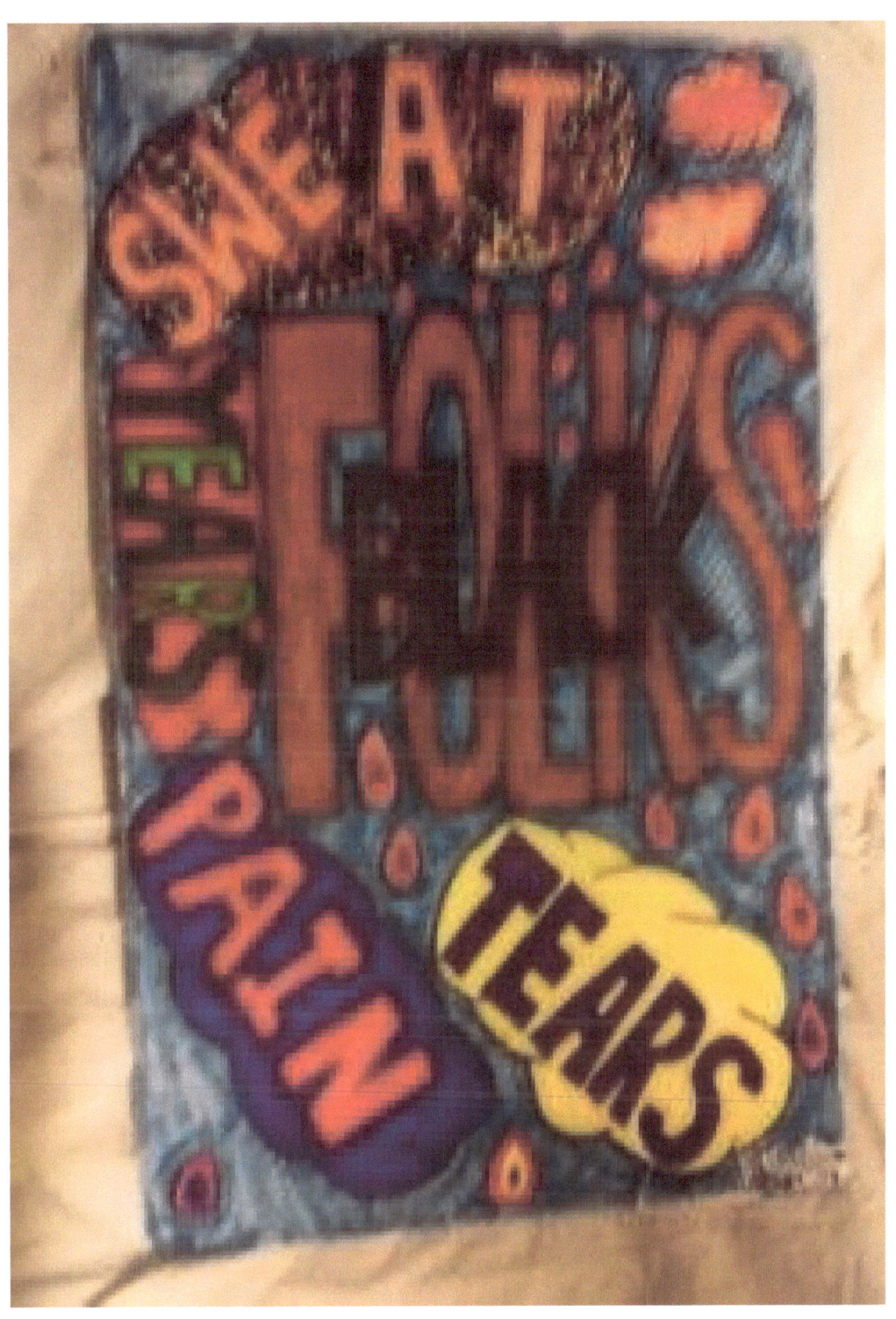

Original Strategy

   This is an original piece of art descriptive of some of the challenges faced historically by Black Folks in an effort to encourage more continued survival and contributions.

It further is a pictorial reflection of the humbling blood, sweat, tears and a call for reciprocal humility in humanity. The bright and lively colors of this original piece attempts to reach the viewer's acknowledgement that these experiences did occur but healing is still needed. It also speaks to the thought that Black Lives in all humanity matters.

Lastly, this original piece speaks to the opportunity to do something about those lessons learned from those gruesome experiences encountered.

Original Art
(Cultural Ball)

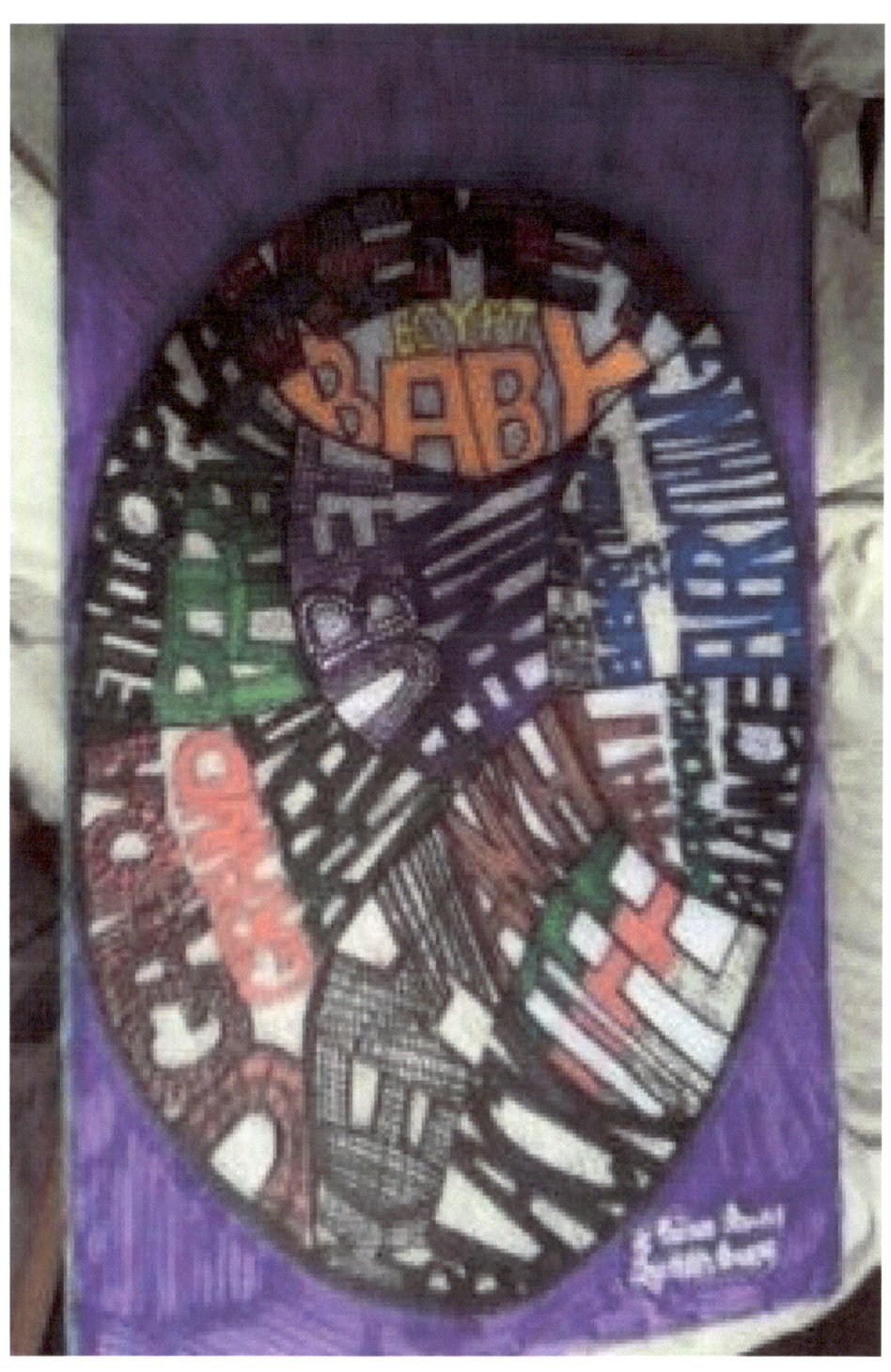

Original Strategy

This concept is designated to bring about a more favorable positive perception towards the human experience regarding black folks. This particular blackball piece of original art highlights a higher prioritized view of a strategy based on favorable ancient concepts. These concepts and relative information can be used as foundation for needed fundamental soundness for challenges today.

It includes momentum brought forward from a unified concept of the continent of what is typically known as Afrika or Africa. This colorful and informational pictorial reflection brings this momentum to surface in all sincerity.

Original Art
(Do Something)

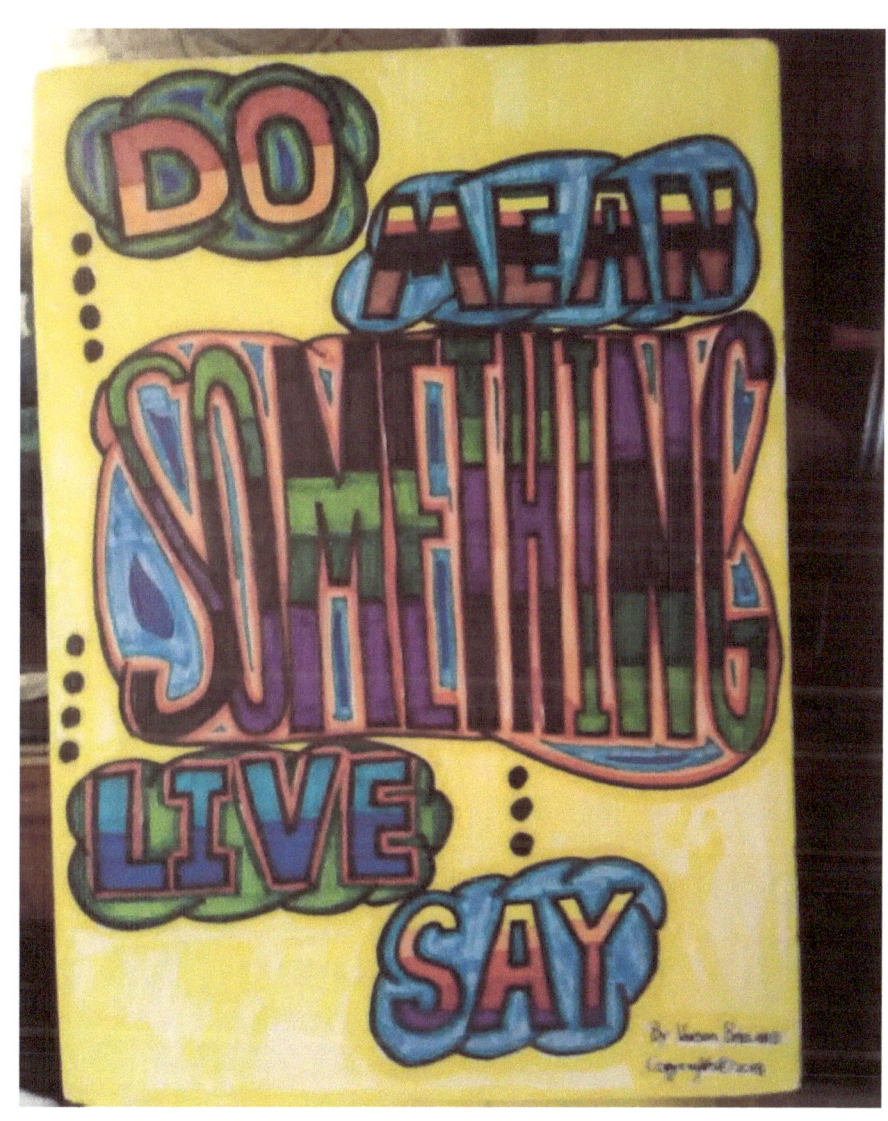

Original Strategy

This speaks to the willing participant existing in such a way that favorable encouragement as a strategy to wisely participate in their life's mission through these principles is necessary. These principles of favorable encouragement are as follows: Do something, mean something, live something and say something. In that regard, this original strategy doesn't include being fragmented or disenfranchised, but it speaks to the individual being as complete and harmonious in their actions as best can be.

Original Art
(It Counts)

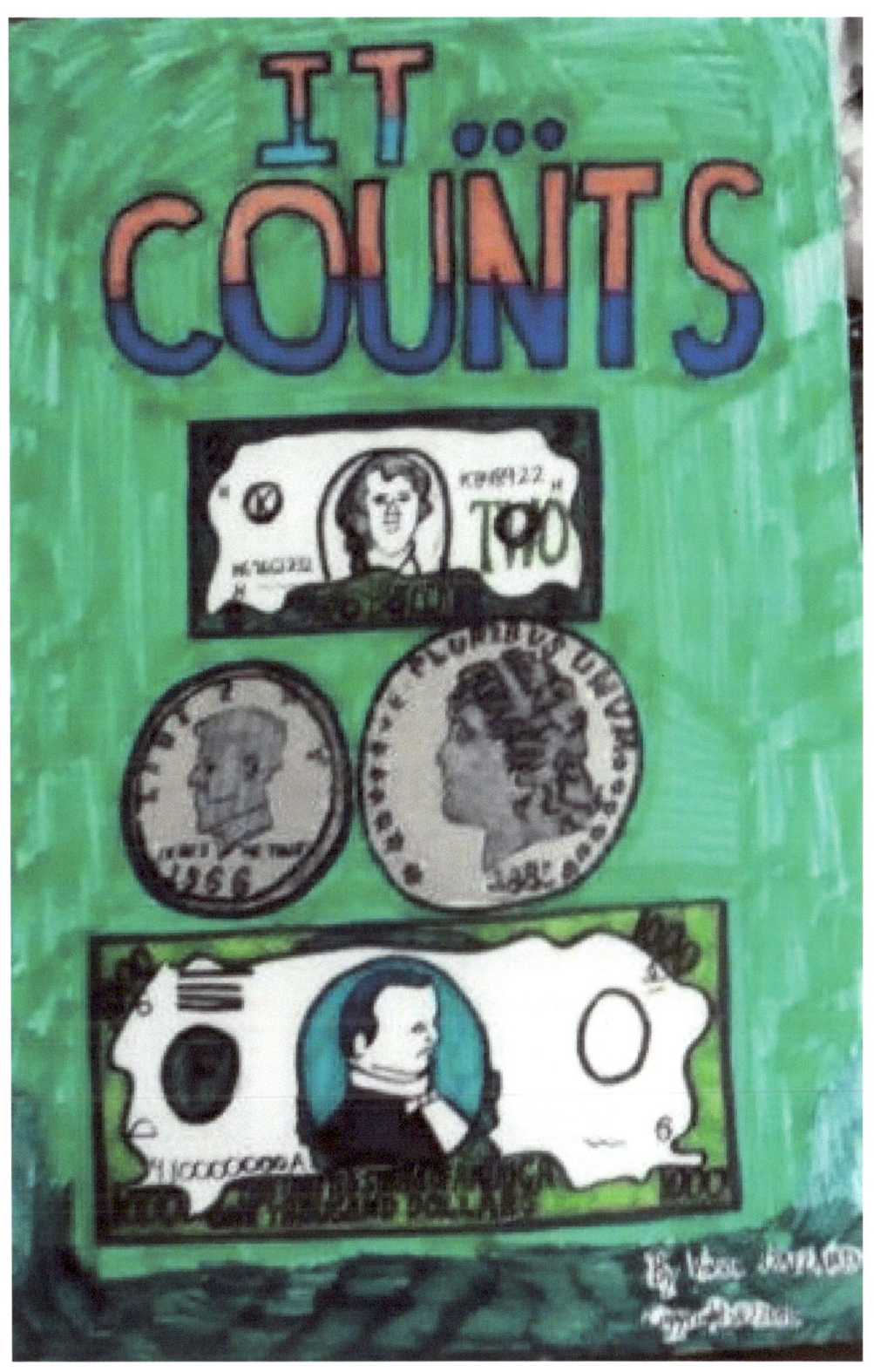

Original Strategy

This original piece of art speaks to the reality of economics and the dynamics that exist in all humanity for it to take place. Equally to be considered is the various acknowledgements of paper monies and coin money in this process. The prestige of those individuals placed on the particular authorized monies is also relative to who is in control and the aim of society in that particular manner.

Chapter Three (3) Family Dynamics

Chapter three on the other hand takes issue with the thought of family dynamics and how it relates to the combining thoughts of Humanitarian Contributions and Racial Reconciliation. Certainly individuals come from family and the dynamics involved brings about the nuts and bolts necessary for family members to survive individually and collectively. Therefore, this certainly puts reality and presence into who actually is doing what, and reaches out to whom and who's that carry out the awesome humanitarian contributions. It also proceeds with the momentum that can dare to have the possibility for bringing about the possible favorable racial reconciliation as this publication suggest that is needed.

Listings

1. Freedom
2. Black Cool
3. Ankh Life
4. Little Girl
5. Son in Sun

Original Art
(Freedom)

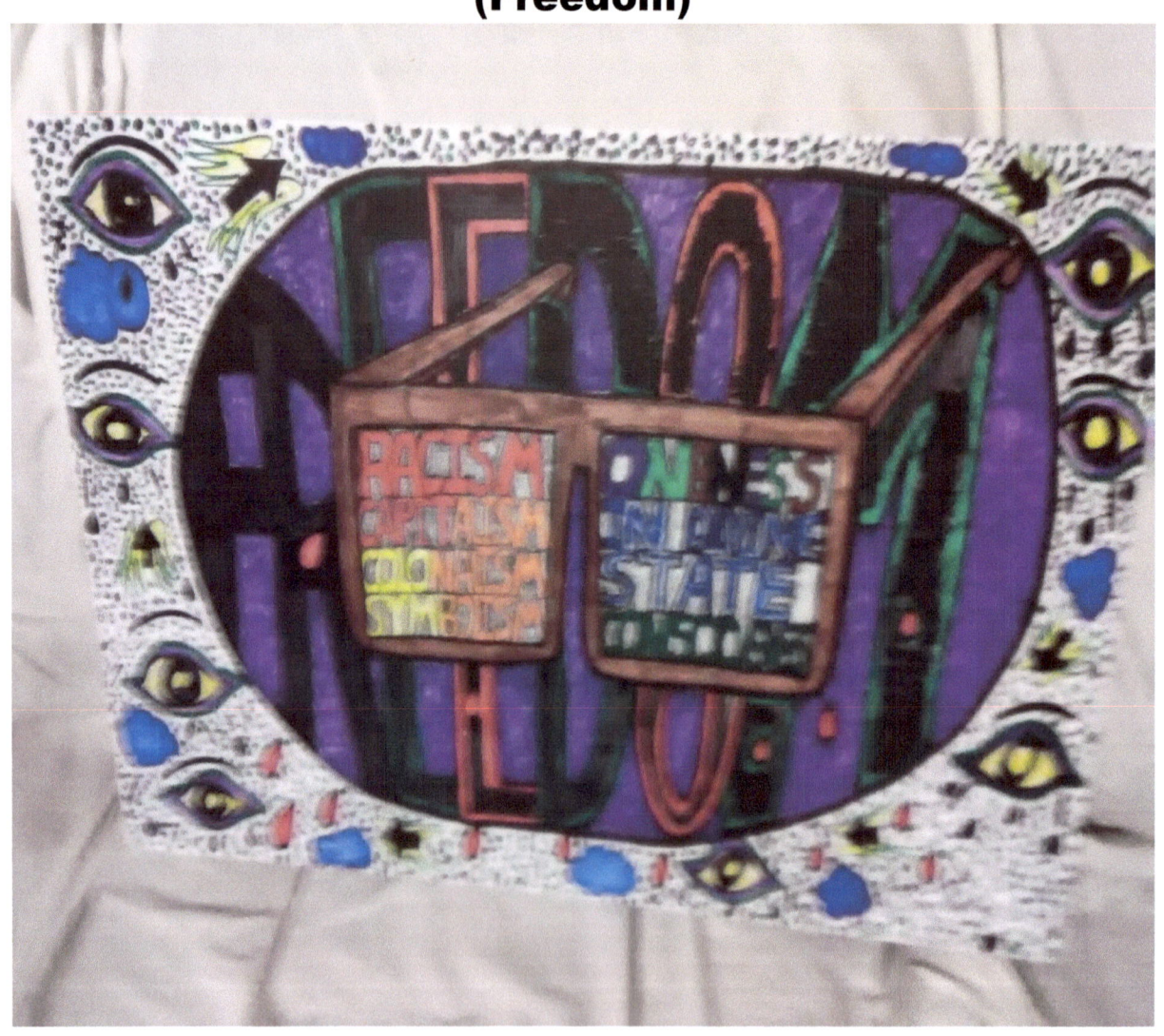

Original Strategy

This speaks to a more favorable look at freedom and its connection to the plight of Black Folks. The glasses creatively bring focus to some views of freedom and its dehumanizing challenges. The challenges mentioned involves: racism, capitalism, colonialism and symbolism. Some favorable resources and strategies includes: oneness, individual in a divine state and consciousness.

Original Art
(Black Cool)

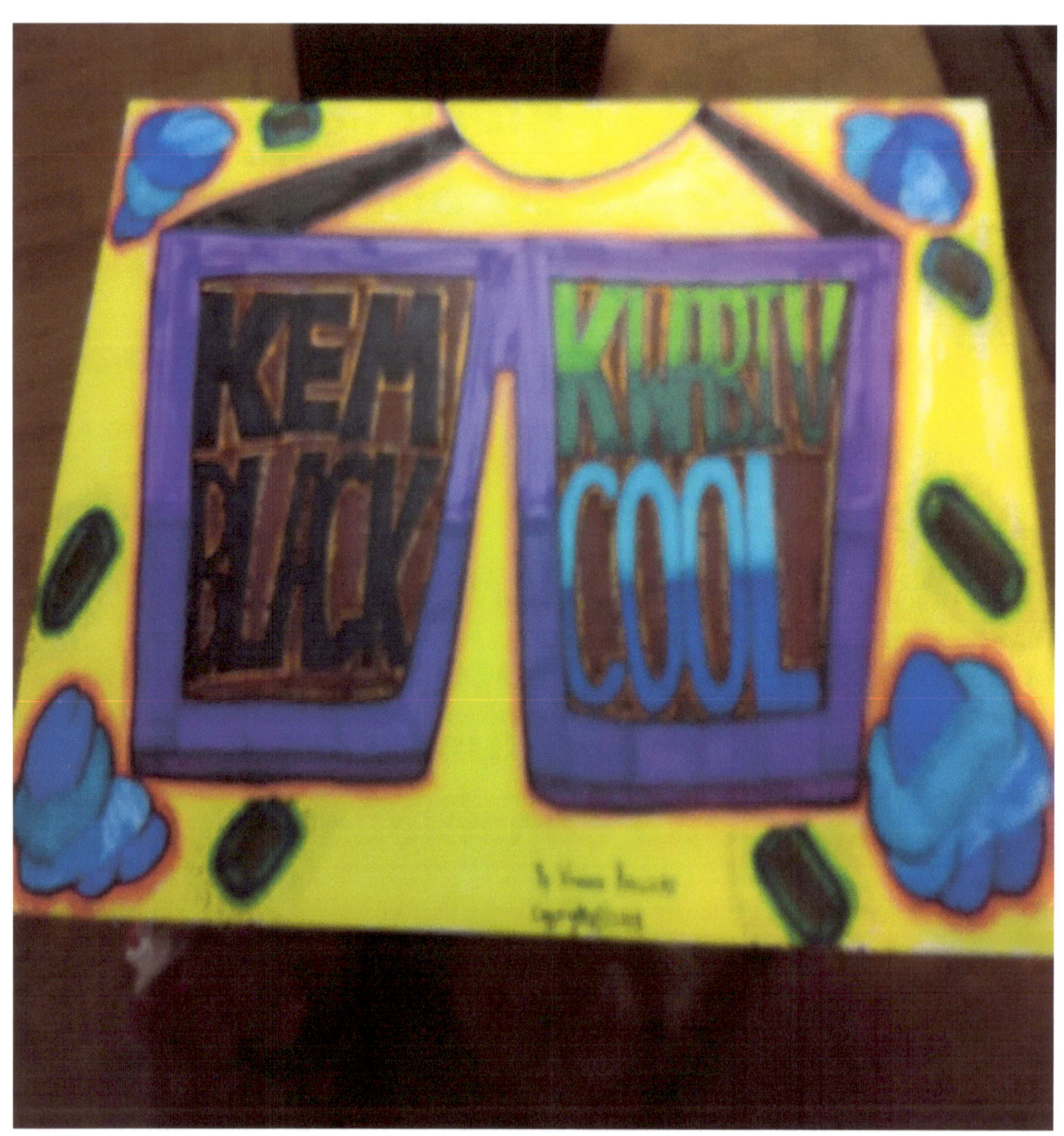

Original Strategy

This original piece of art speaks to the awesome tolerance and dignity that those individuals of what is typically identified as Black folks have brought to the surface regarding humanitarian contributions. A further focus here is how those individuals have shown remarkable calmness and coolness while making some of these awesome humanitarian contributions as referenced.

This piece further speaks to a bilingual kind of cultural display to bring the point of focus across accordingly. From the classical language of Medu Netcher and presently the English language are the two that focus the point of Black Cool or coolness. Kem in the classical language of Medew Netcher deals with the naming the color of black, and Kwabiv is the English transliteration for being cool in MDW Netcher. Therefore, this creatively and colorfully brings these concepts to the surface in an encouraging manner.

Original Life
(Ankh Life)

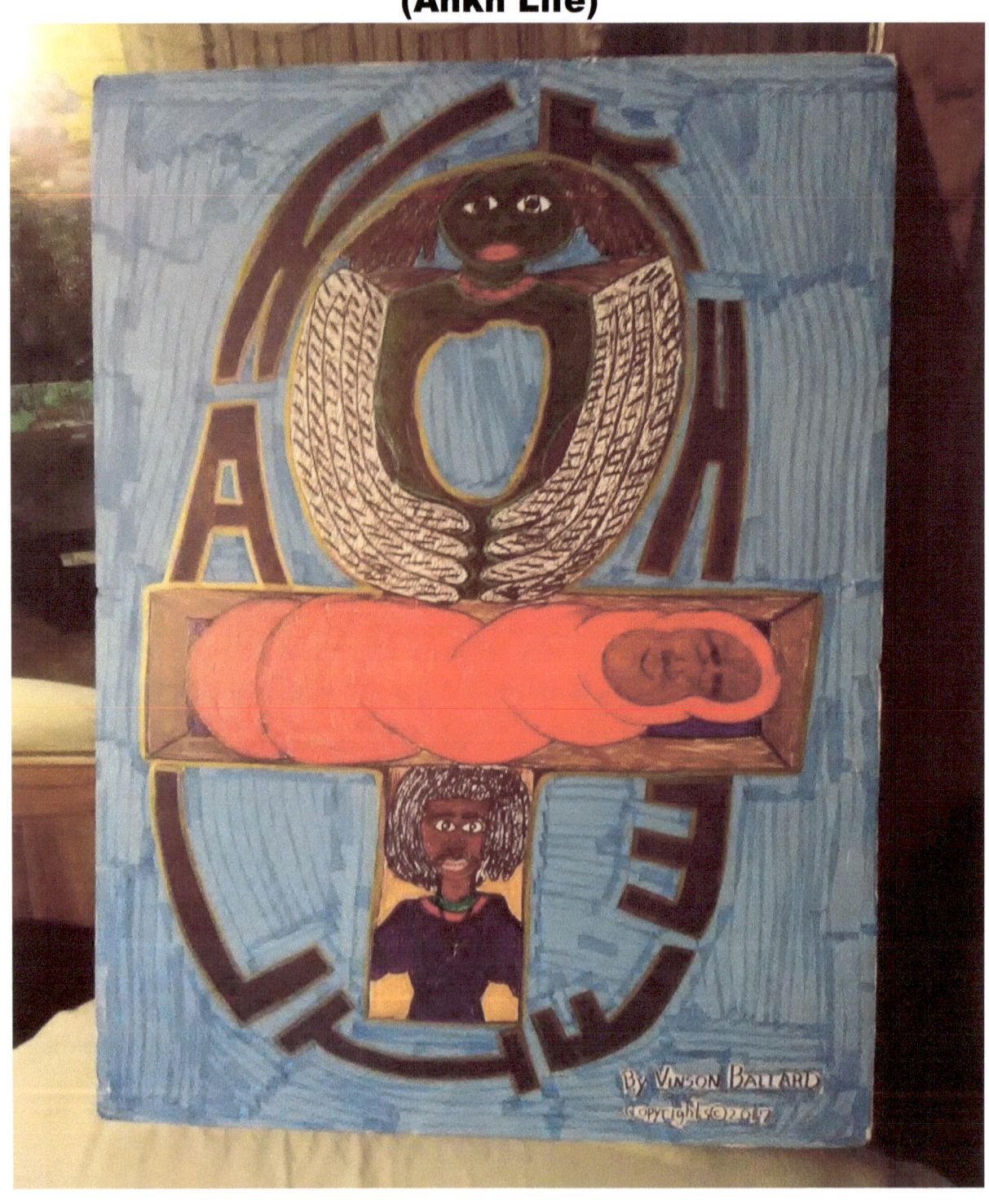

Original Strategy

This brings forward a strategy from a higher prioritized cultural perspective. It further emphasizes the importance of the divine humane family experience from a divine universal consciousness perspective. It involves the universal divine role of the mother/ woman shown with wings, and the father/ male. On the original piece of art, the male is shown connecting at the bottom of the ankh with the intersection in the middle being the birth of the offspring or the child which represents life. The wings of the woman symbolize the flight to an individual pursuing a higher level of spiritual consciousness. The wings are complemented by the energy of the mother and father respectively.

Original Art
(Little Girl)

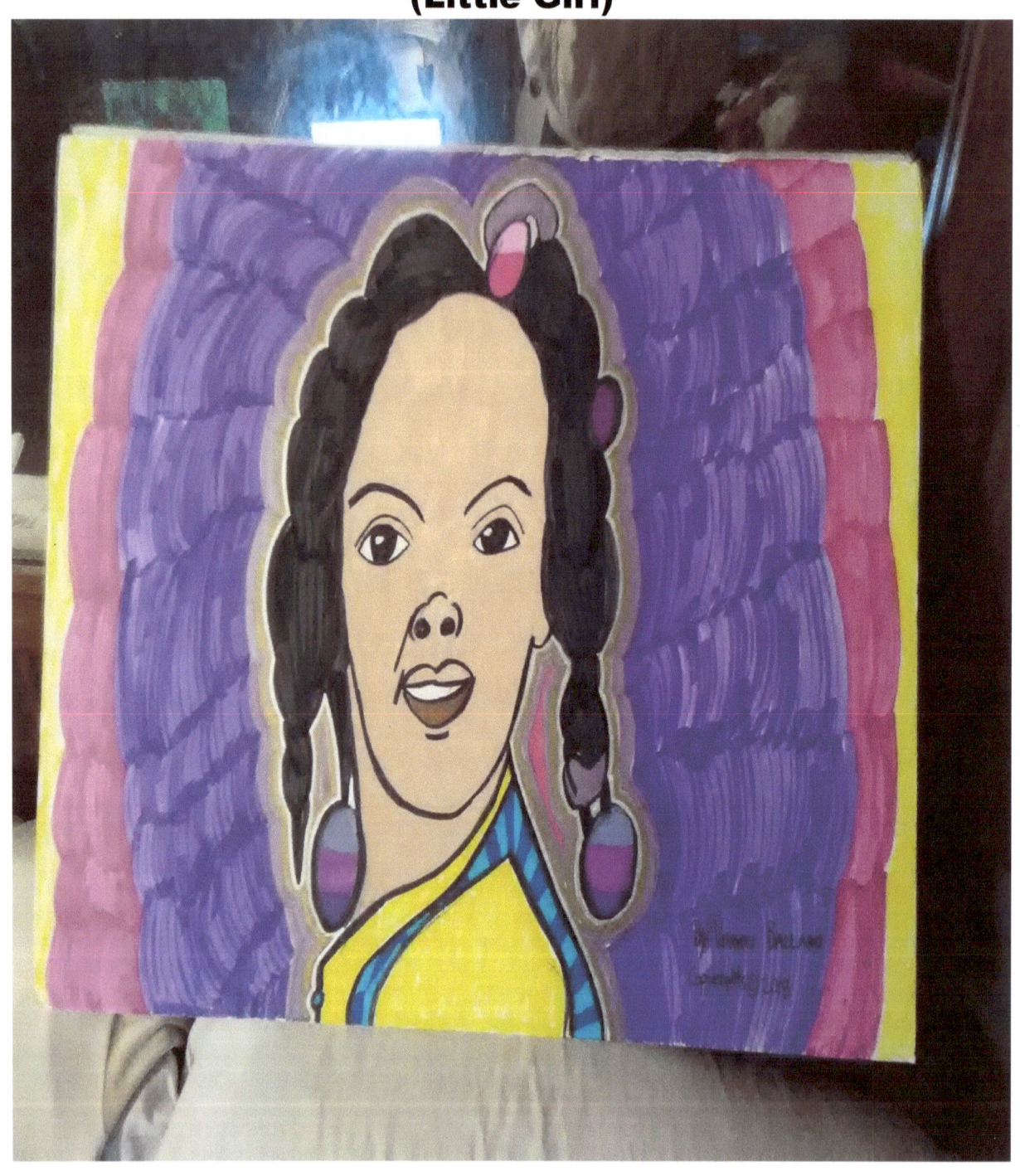

Original Strategy

This is an original picture of a younger female in a family that went through an incident that proved a very undesirable deadly outcome. Therefore, this original piece of art speaks to the need for family participation at the highest priority level for all members. It should most definitely involve a favorable supporting cast for humanitarian contributions to continue and have a chance at even further assisting with the issue of racial reconciliation when necessary.

Original Art
(Son in Sun)

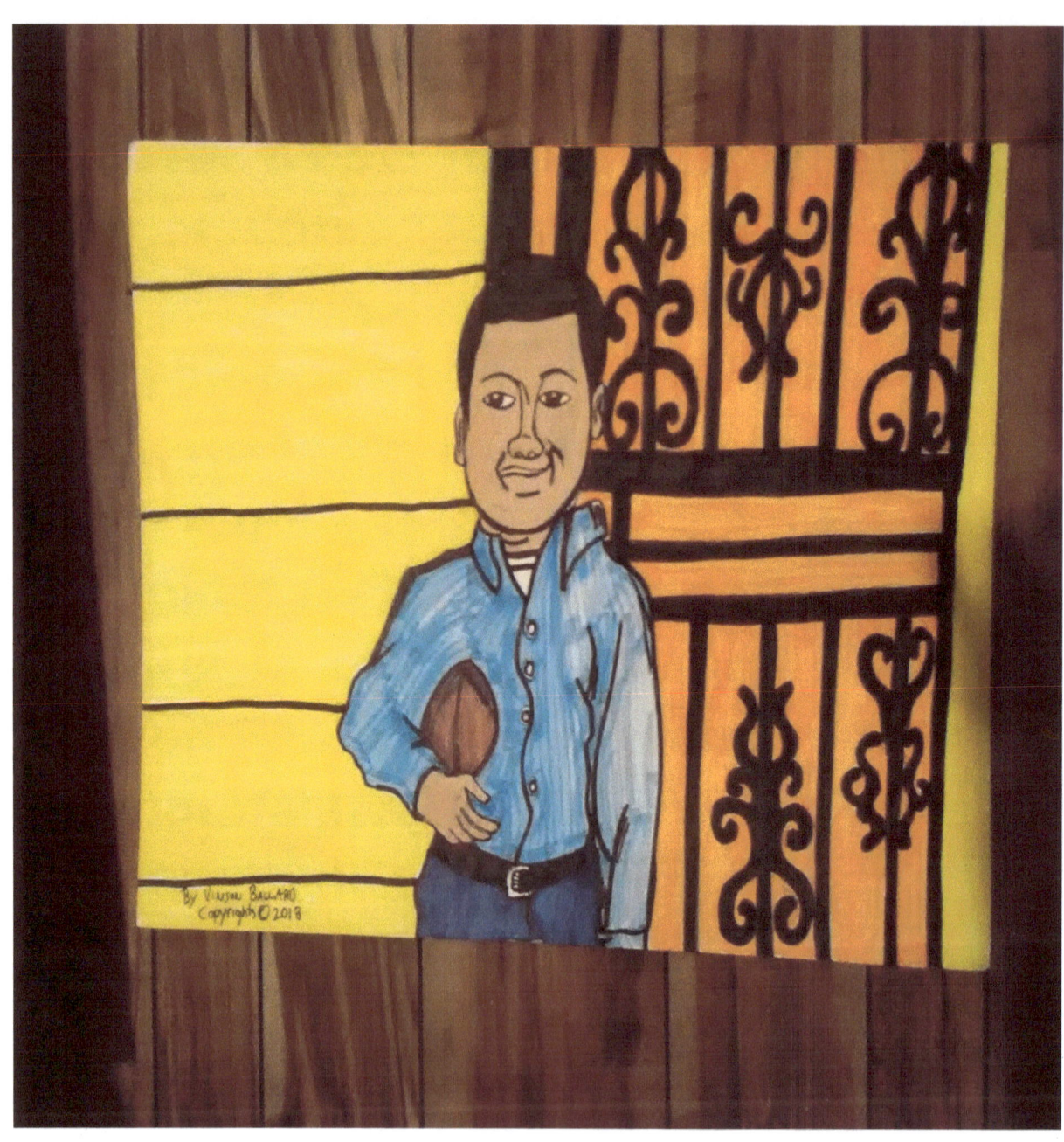

Original Strategy

This original piece of art speaks to a youth standing holding a football by the door of a house. This youth in this particular photo happens to be a young African American male. It also must be brought forward with how the sunlight from the Sun is certainly interacting with the youth in a very positive and favorable way as with the very connecting bright colors in his clothes.

Chapter Four (4)

Reconciliation

Chapter four attempts to further deal with this issue from a standpoint of focusing on the thought of reconciliation in general as the entire publication systematically suggest. Of course within this point of view, there must be some genuine pursuits to include the concepts of reunion, settlement and to make peace as it relates to reconciliation. Perhaps the question could arise in this instance on what grounds and who is in control of that instance and lastly how does the issue of fact finding, primary sources and truth have to do with the reality achieved in actually getting to the point of reconciliation? Certainly, the original listings of art pieces are very much welcomed to bring insight to such an interesting opportunity to deal with this accordingly.

Art Listings

1. MDW NTR Greetings
2. Family Greetings
3. 42 for Life
4. Maat spiral
5. Mississippi
6. See Doctor
7. U Can

Original Art
(Ankh Life)

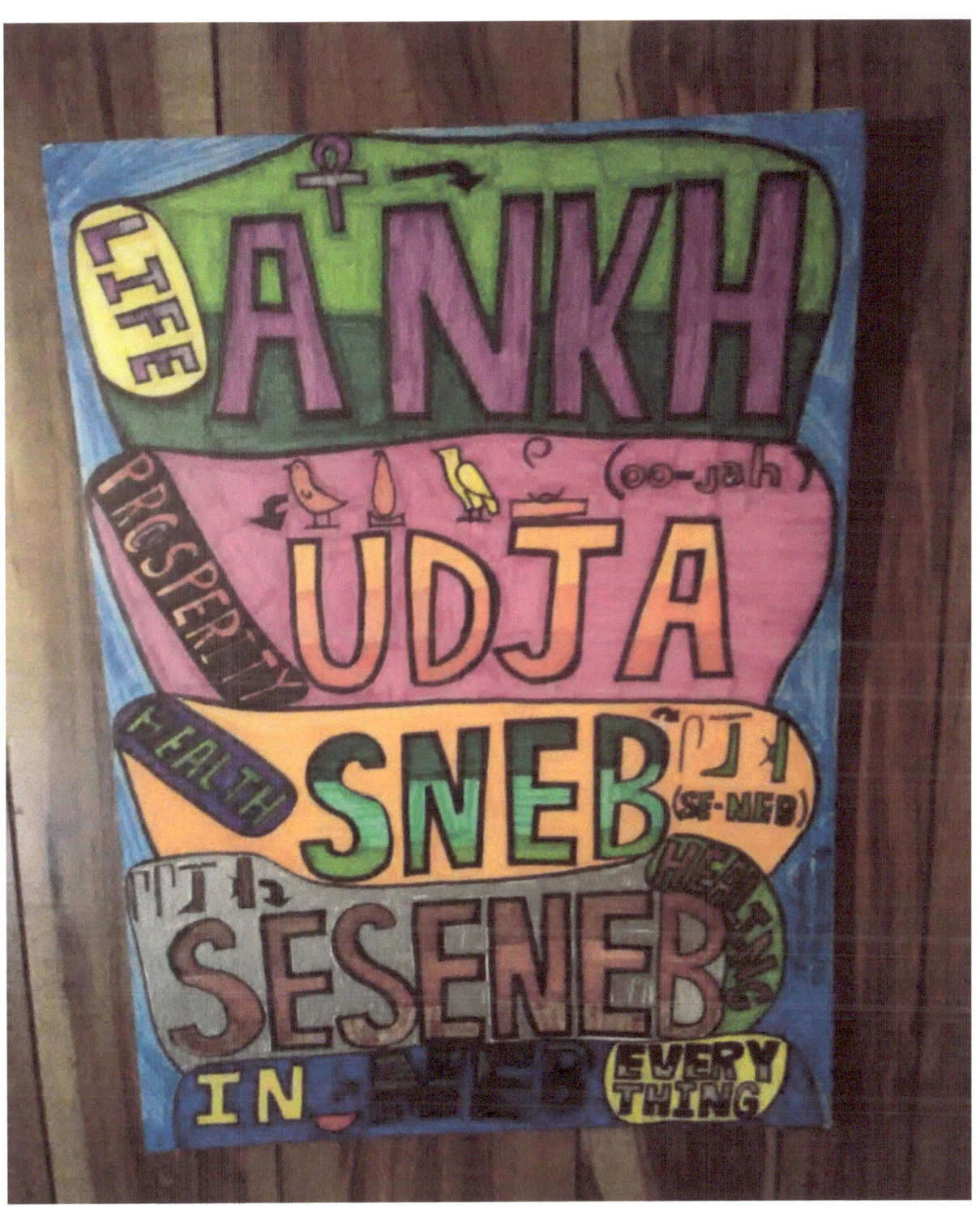

Original Strategy

This is a bilingual pictorial reflection of an ancient greeting from the classical African language of MDW Netcher. It may be viewed from a three - fold perspective. That involves: 1) the Classical African Language of Medew (MDW) Netcher; 2) the English Transliteration and 3) the glyphs or pictorial portrayal of the meaning.

This includes the greeting that is perceived as most favorable in greeting the opposing individual with the characteristics of life, prosperity, health and healing in as a positive way obtainable.

Original Art
(Family Greeting)

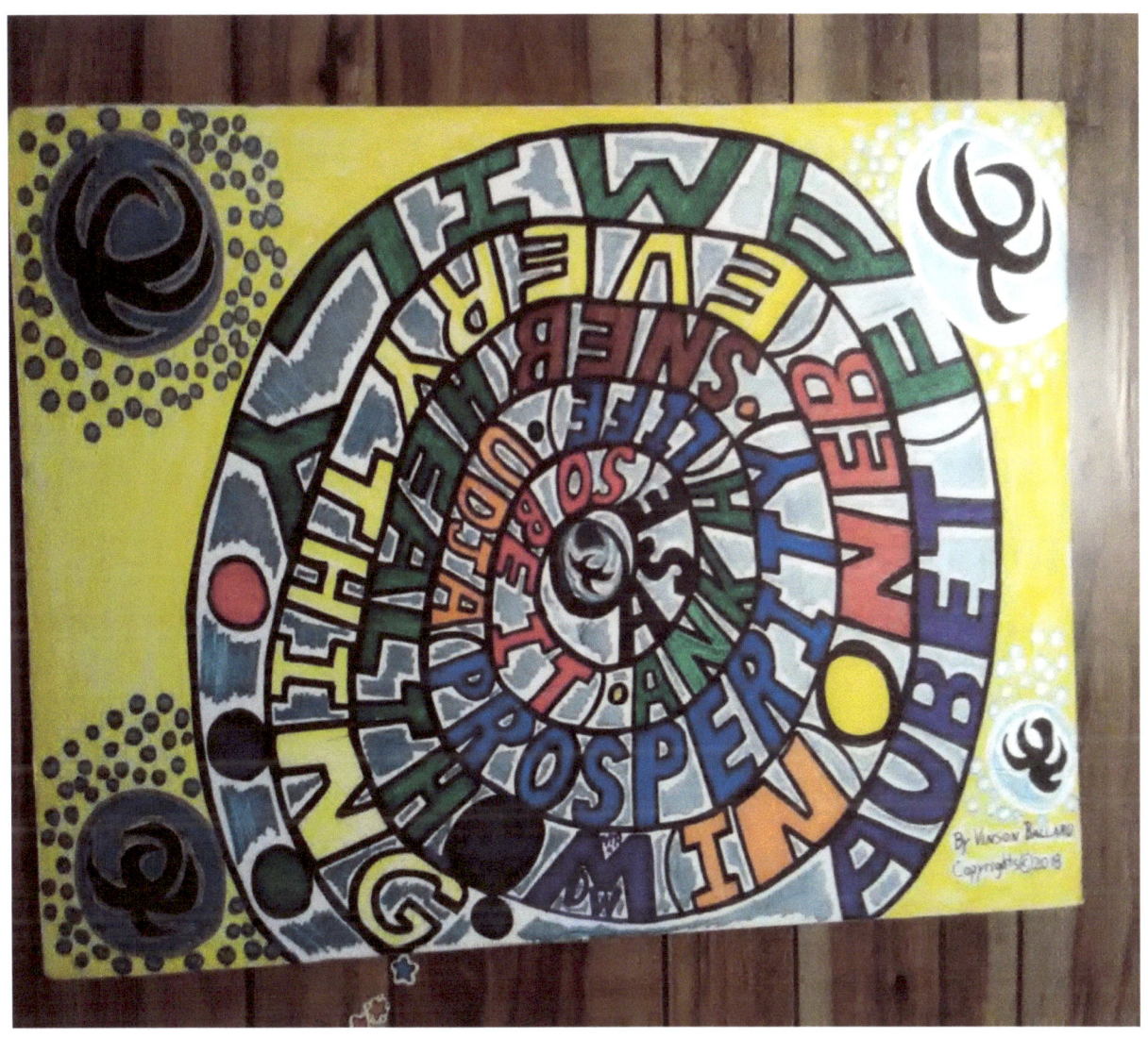

Original Strategy

This original piece of art speaks to a very harmonious family greeting from the ancient language of MDW Netcher. However, it has been brought forward with an English relative attempted meaning in as a best as possible from a truly student perspective. The art piece sets a standard for greeting family and neighbors in a very positive manner. This is done by greeting with a phrase of so be it (Ase'), life (ankh), and prosperity (udja), health (sneb) in everything (neb), family (aubet).

(Original Art)
42 For Life

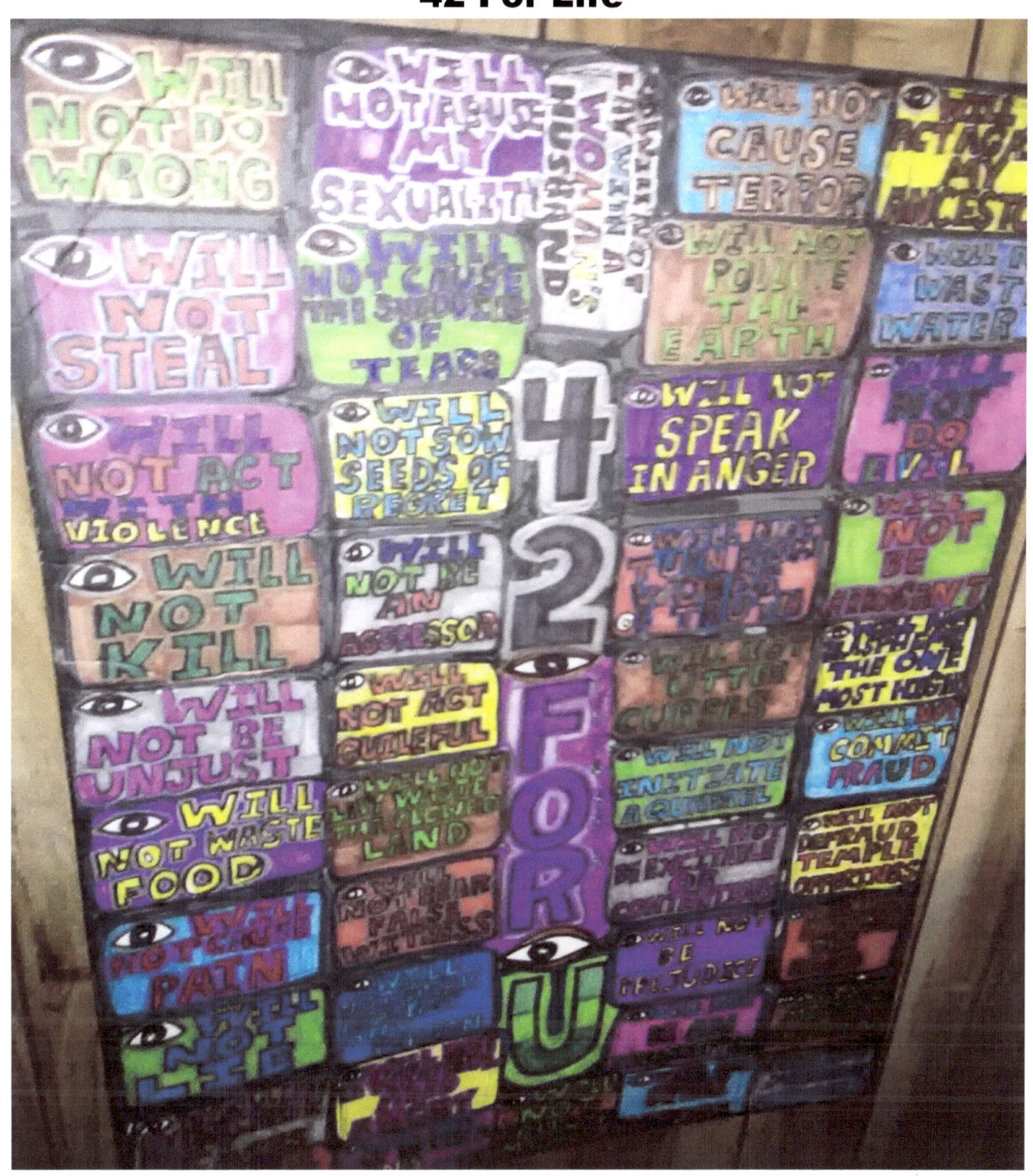

Original Strategy

This speaks to the forty two divine principles of the classical ancient concept of Maat (Harmonious Balance) that individuals are supposed to live by in their everyday daily life experiences.

Original Art
(Maat Spiral)

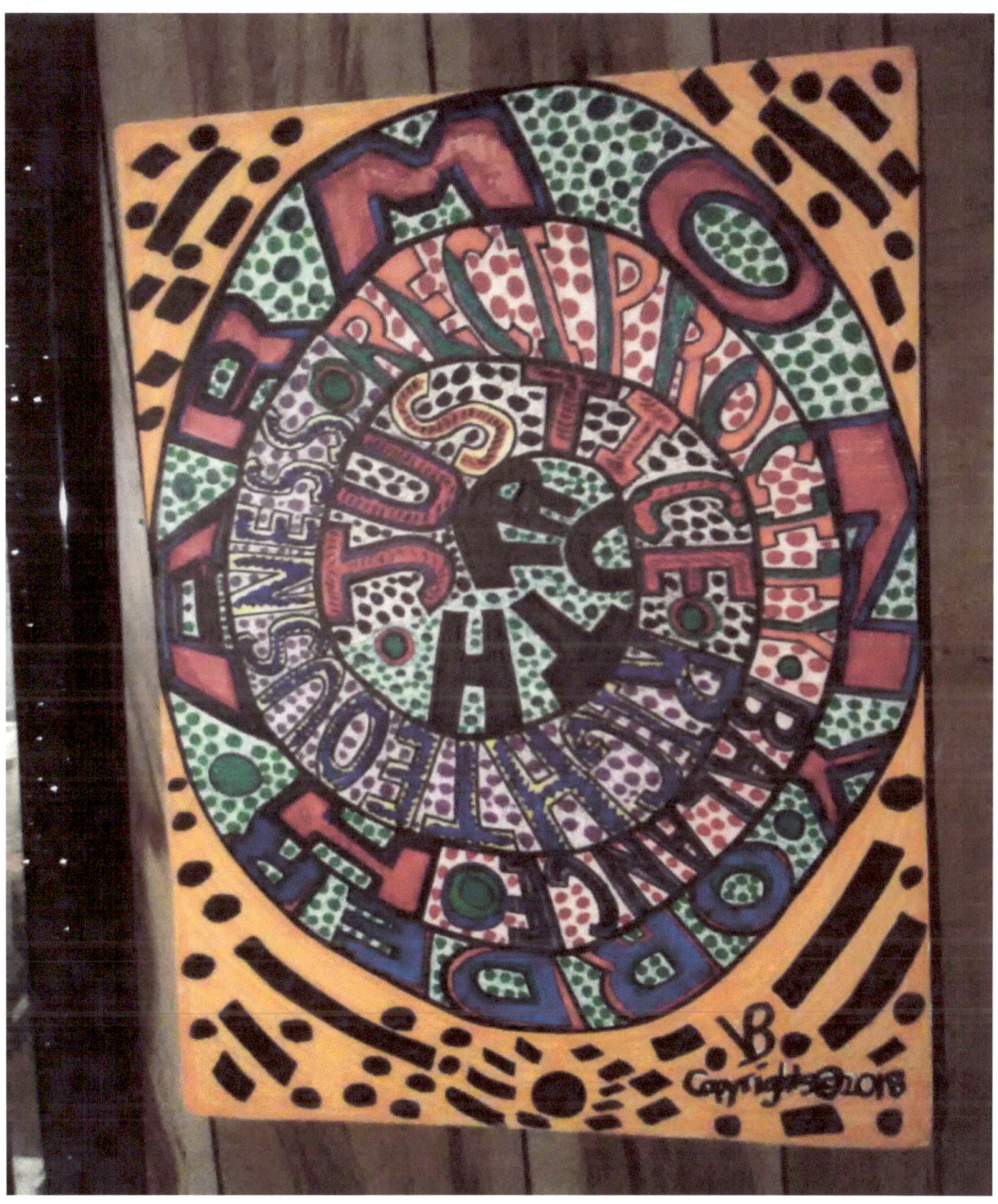

Original Strategy

This original piece of art gives a creative view of the ancient concept of Maat. It further brings this to surface with a more in depth look within the characteristics of Maat from a progressive spiral perspective. It certainly progresses from the standpoint of its benchmarks of truth, justice, righteousness, reciprocity, balance, harmony and order. It also symbolizes the basic importance that the concept makes readily available for the willing participant and/ or reader.

(Original Art)
Mississippi

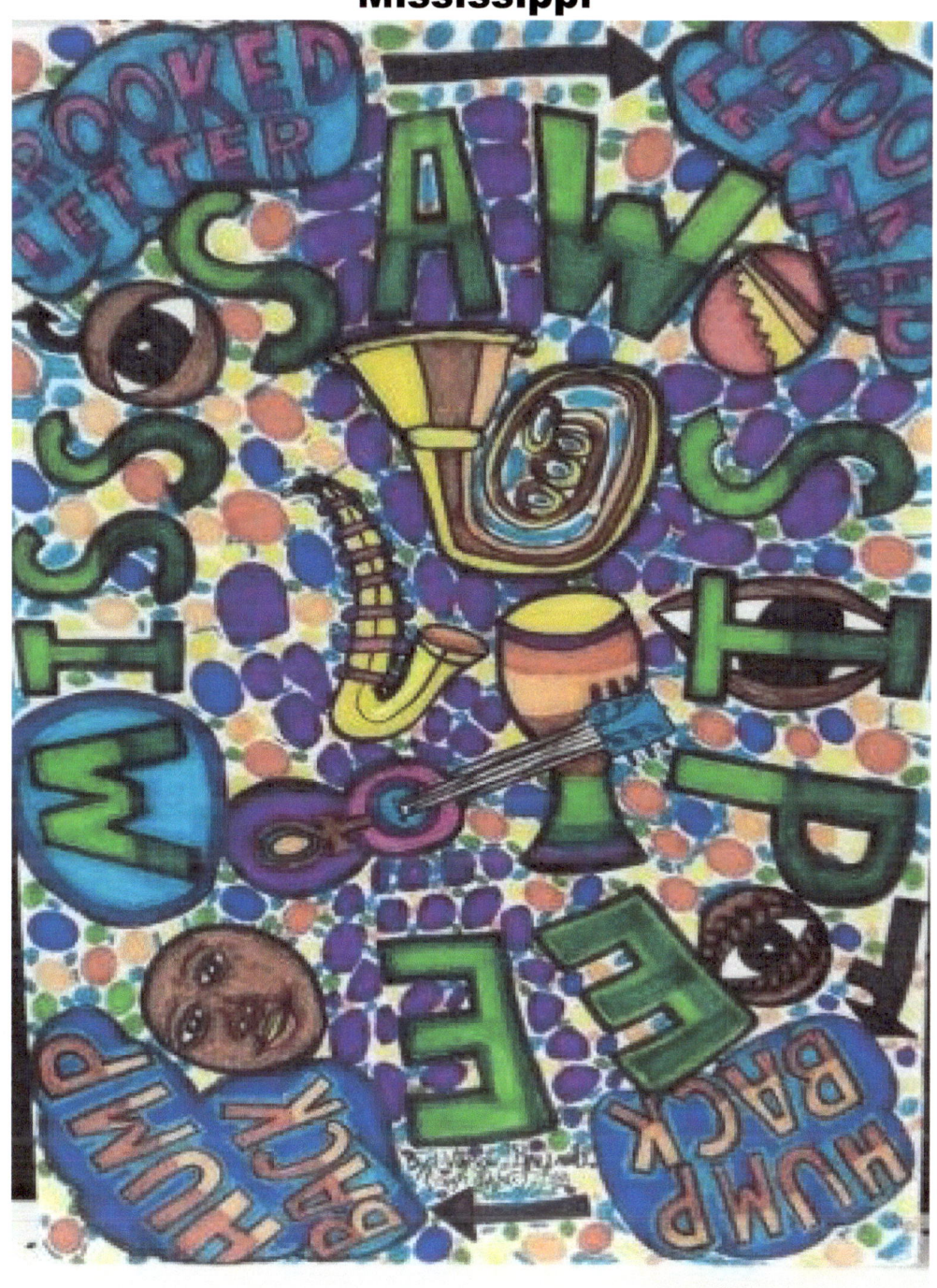

Original Strategy

This original piece of art speaks to the unique culture of the geographical location in the southern part of the United States of America in a creative way. The culture is noted as being universal and it is not limited to one particular area of focus.

Original Art
(See Doctor)

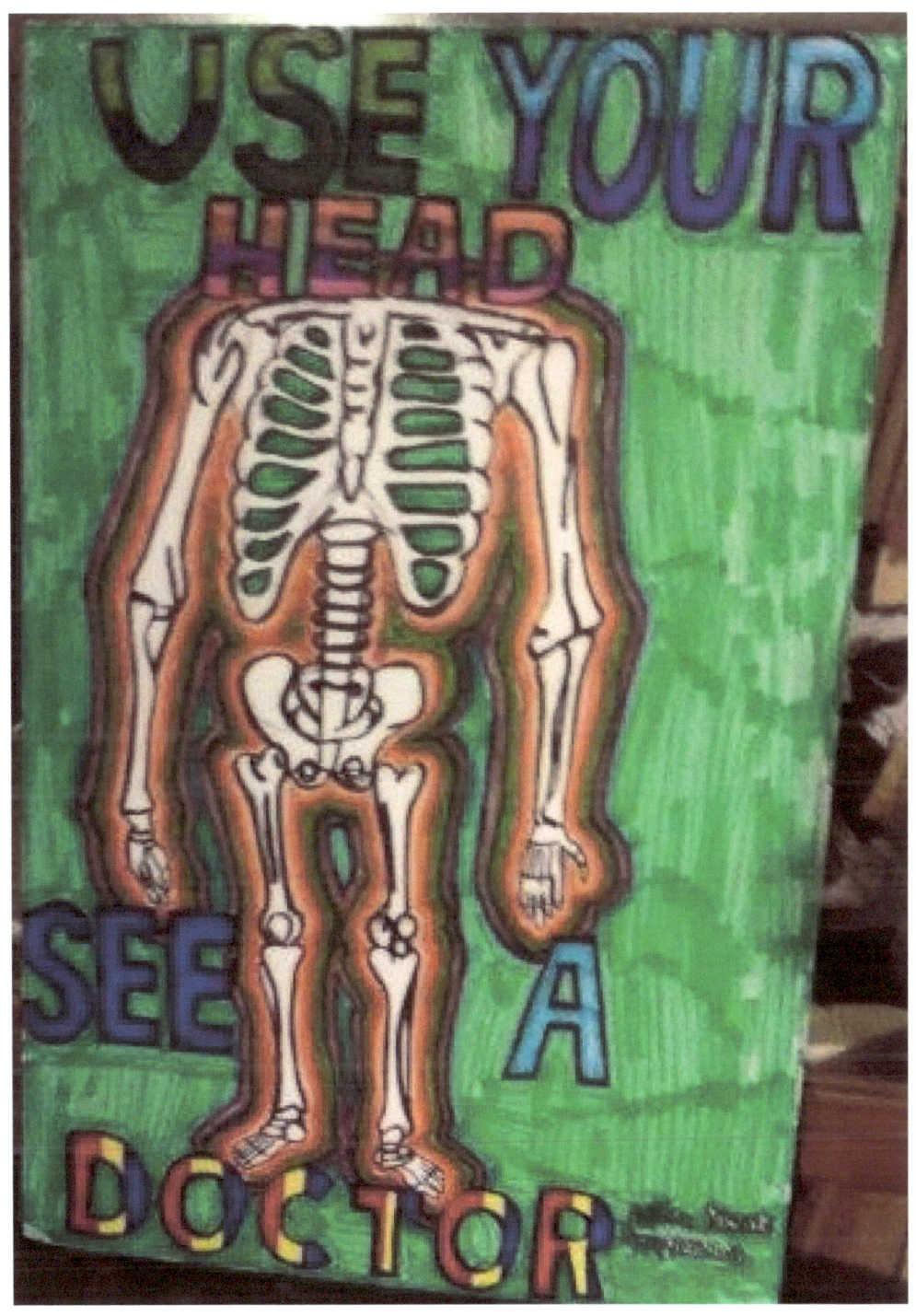

Original Strategy

This original piece of art speaks to the concept of the willing participant favorably striving to achieve the best individual state of wellness as best and wise as possible. Of course, this involves health, spirituality and its divine dynamics in the best possible way towards survival.

Original Art
(U Can)

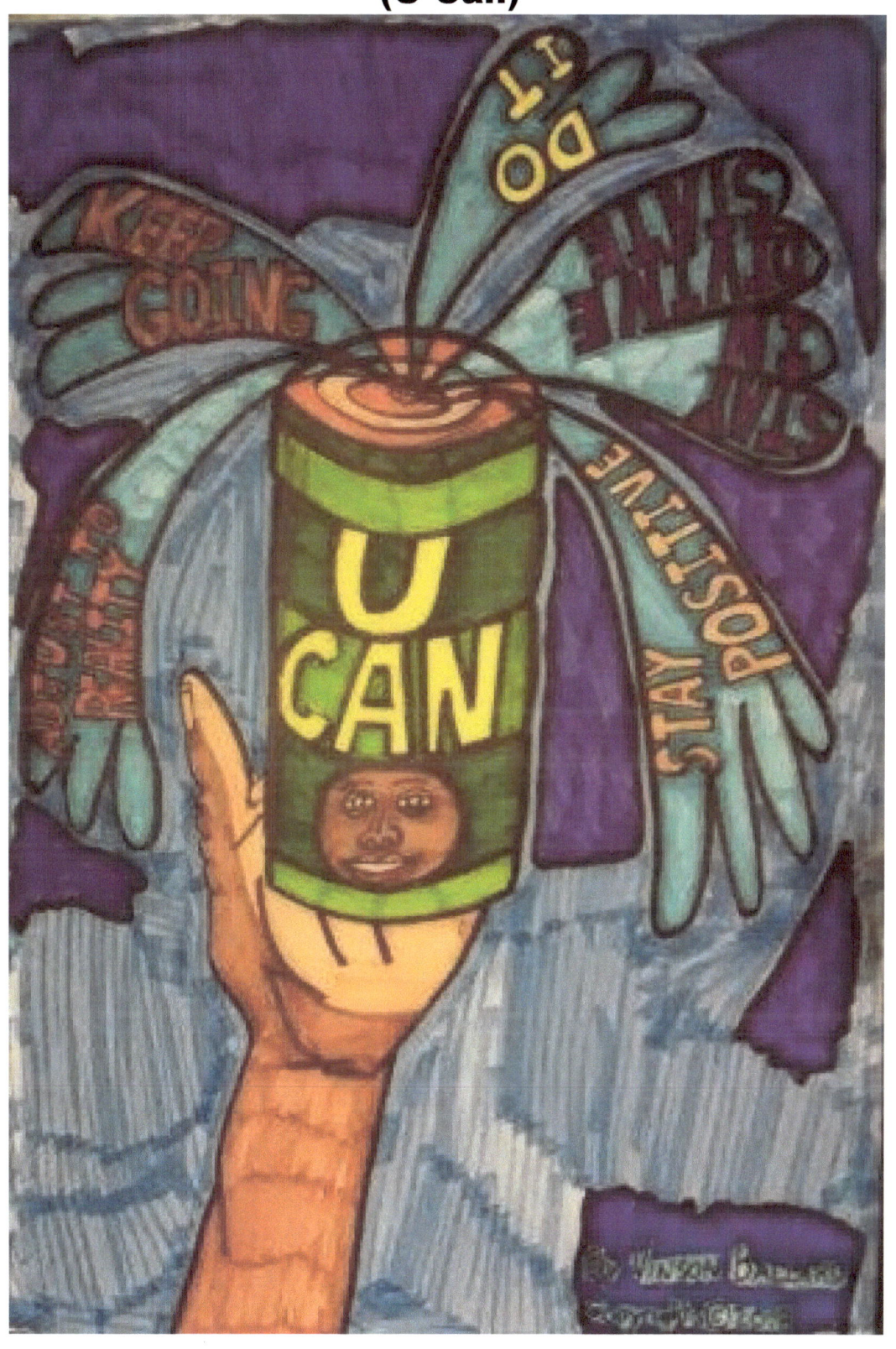

Original Strategy

This original piece of art encourages the individual to keep existing in as a wiser and best way possible. It begins this by centering its efforts on the concept of the individual can or in particular "u can." Some other relative supporting parts of the strategy are as follows: 1) Adjust to reality, 2) keep going, 3) do it, 4) stay in your divine state and 5) stay positive;

Chapter Five (5)

Putting It Together

Chapter five is the final chapter of this publication and it attempts to bring closure within this effort by simply putting it all together. Therefore, none of the previous chapters should be viewed as fragmented or unrelated, but they should be very much connected with as relative and fitting on a case by case basis. Therefore, the concepts of contributing (chapter one), humanitarian 101 (chapter two), family dynamics (chapter three), reconciliation (chapter four) shall be put together to place the polishing touches on this original publication as a whole suggest.

Original Art Listings

1. Band Aid (Heal)
2. TWA
3. 2 – 3 (Green)
4. 2 – 3 (Vert.)
5. 3 – D

Original Art/ Band Aid

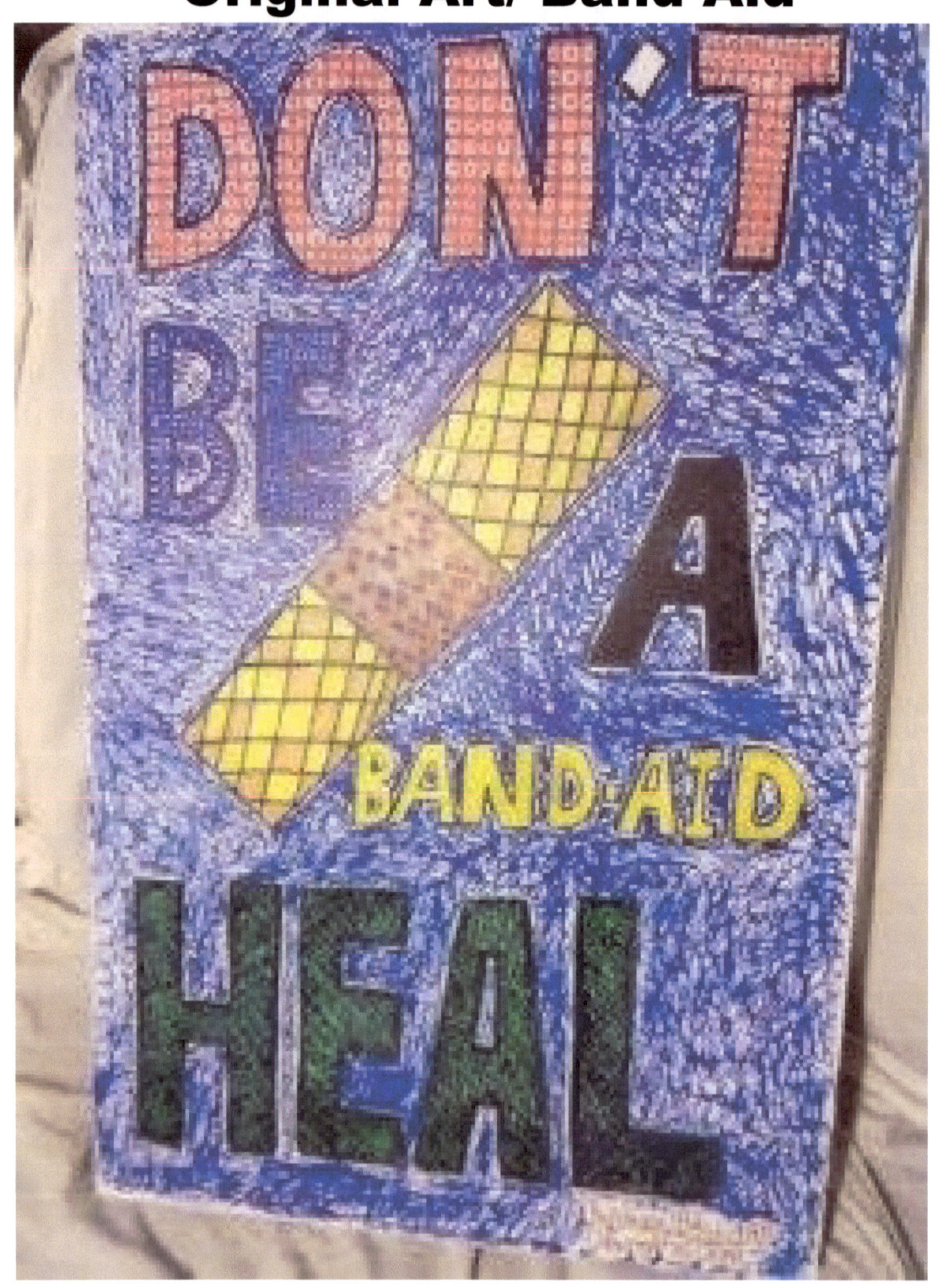

Original Strategy

This original art piece speaks to encouraging the reader to actively participant in replenishing; restoring and making their self to get better towards continued survival. The band aid acknowledgement speaks to the individual only limiting their self to a temporarily. It also empowers the willing participant and reader to get better, in as a wiser, higher prioritized manner possible.

Original Art
(TWA)

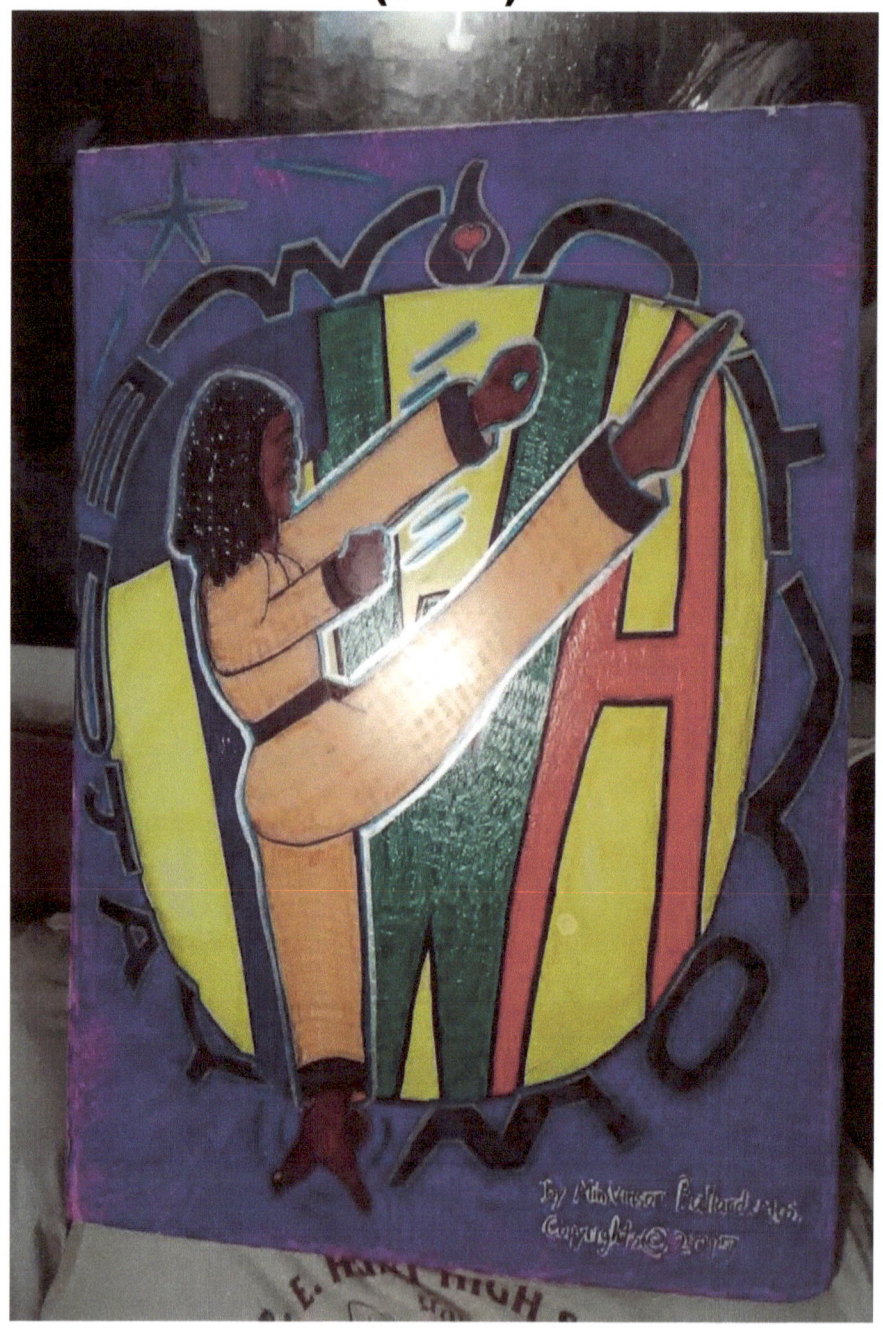

Original Strategy

This original piece of art brings favorable insight to the earlier ancient concept of discipline. It highlights a reference to an ancient group of black folks called the Twa people. This is documented in an ancient primary source called the Famine Stela. It also reference an elite well trained group of warriors called the Medjay. The final reference includes that of an earlier name of the present day combat system called Montu (earlier Mentu). In that regard, the reader or willing participant is provided with awesome cultural examples of why it is sometimes necessary to grasp the notion of discipline in the wiser more higher prioritized way possible.

Original Art
(2 – 3)

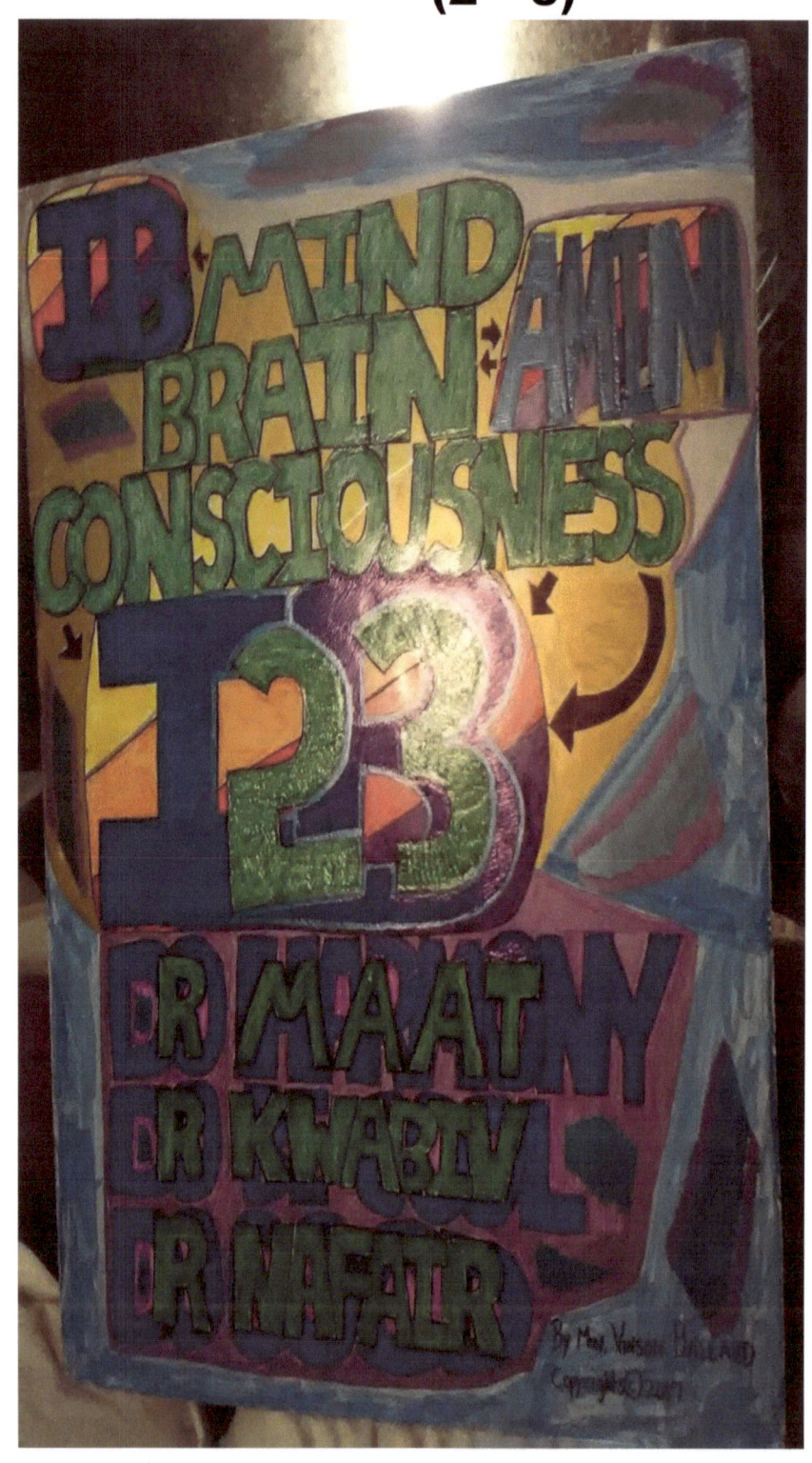

Original Strategy

This is a higher prioritized recommended cultural strategy for the willing participant and reader. It comes from a bilingual interpretation which consist as follows: 1) staying focused by way of the mind (ib), brain (amim), consciousness (ib) as the first three of the two three.

The second concept of the two three may be found as follows: 1 (do balanced harmony – R maat in the classical language of MDW Netcher; 2 (do be cool – R Kwabiv in MDW Netcher and 3 (do good, beautifulness, happiness) and R nafair in MDW Netcher. This strategy is recommended through a cultural combination as with the 2 – 3 concept for the willing participant / reader.

Original Art
(2 – 3)

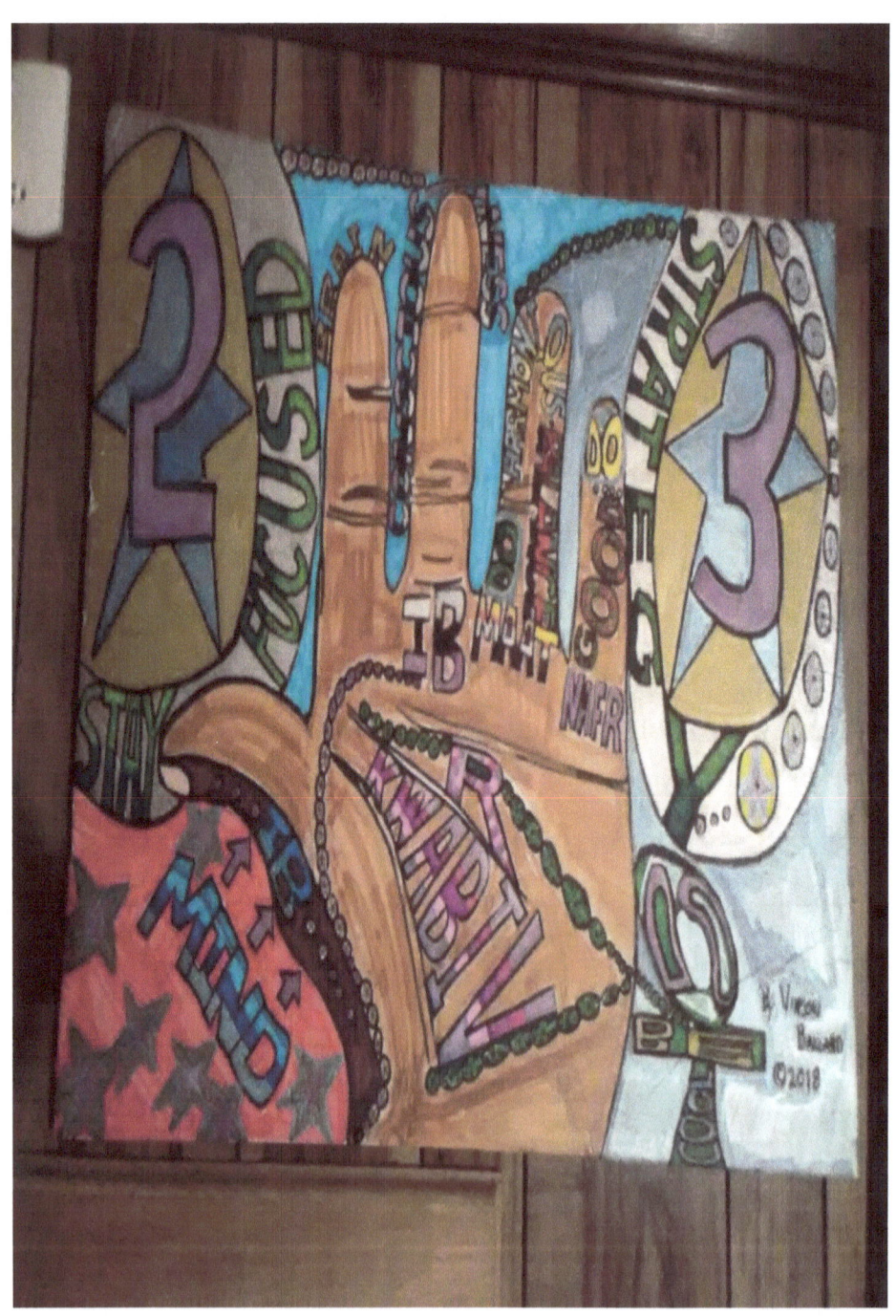

Original Strategy

This is another continuous replica of the Two Three (2 – 3) Concept. It brings a closer focus by way of it being a hand full because two plus three is five. Of course, five is actually the hand full that this original piece brings to the surface in all sincerity. The first two of the two three has to do with staying focused as with using your mind, brain and consciousness. The second two has to do with bring to the surface a more workable strategy with three portions. This involves doing harmonious balance, doing being good, beautiful, happy and using one's youthfulness. In all, this strategy certainly offers the willing participant a wonderful strategy for survival.

Original Art
(3 – D)

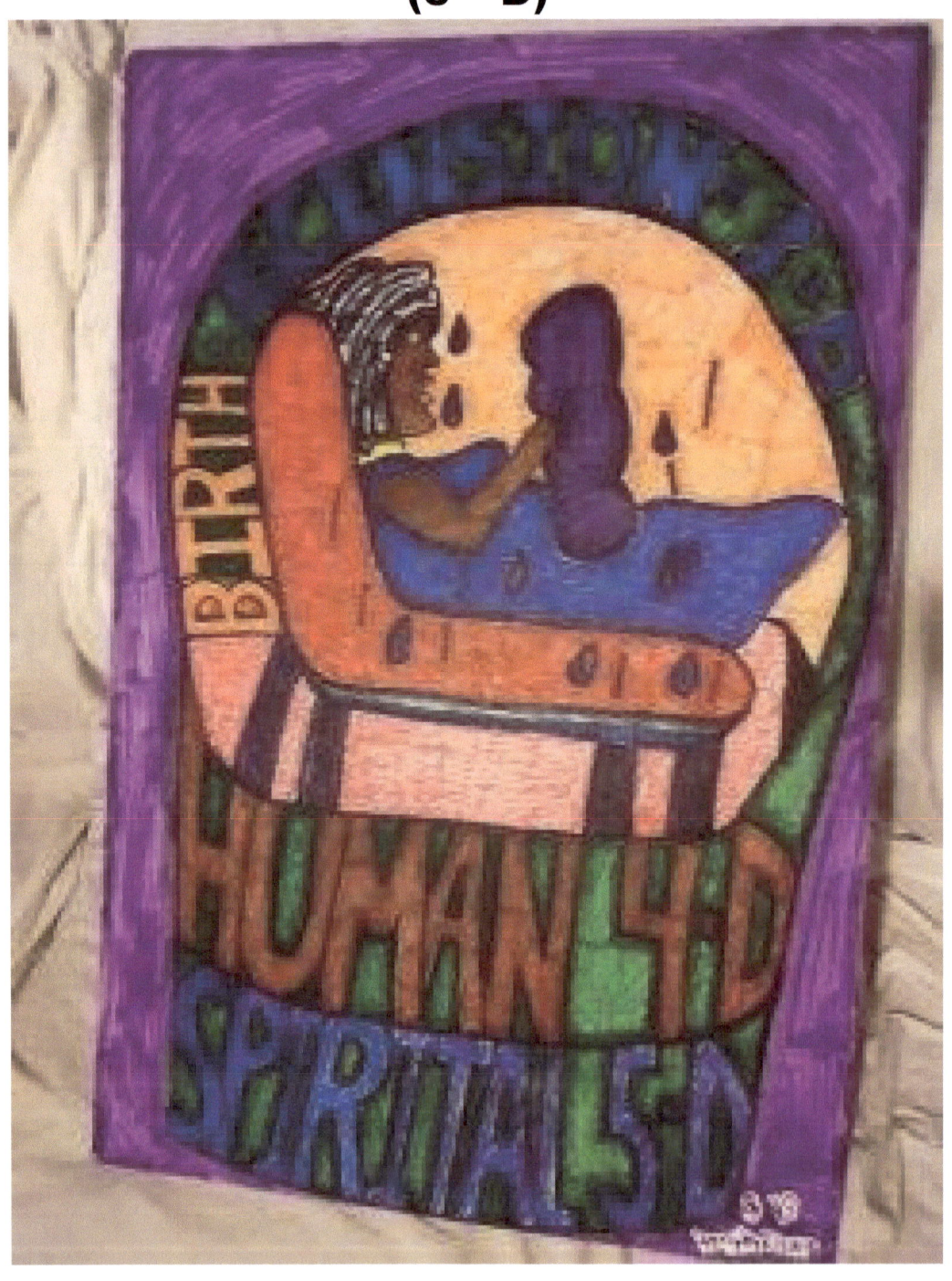

Original Strategy

This original piece of art speaks to the divine reality of the divine creation during the birth process as a divine creation. This focus also reflects the importance of the development and growth of the youth during this process. It also emphasizes how the offspring is ascending at birth to the third domain/ dimension and must further through and to the fourth (human domain) and the fifth domain (higher spirit consciousness).

Conclusion

There could be other important realities to gather about the topic of humanitarian contributions and racial reconciliation. In that humble regard, I have attempted to come from a genuine out of the box perspective in bringing forth some information that possibly would not surface otherwise. Of course, surface otherwise here simply refers to how certain aspects of the mainstream population would not produce such a cultural kind of publication as I have brought forward.

Certainly take notice to the references where I suggest that the willing participant go to search for the relative and/ or contributing information that deals with issues that the original artwork and relative strategies brings to the surface during this publication. Remember, all of the chapters, the relative acknowledged art work and strategies individually and collectively bring an uncovered reality about art that touches home. These concepts bring forward this intended energy that deals with the subject of humanitarian contributions in an original creative way that can be very beneficial if pursued in a fitting way on a case by case basis.

Summary of Original Art Page Listing

Healing Warrior Sun	**p.10**
Consciousness	**p. 13**
Good Behavior	**p. 15**
Smile	**p. 17**
Who Will Honor their Role	**p. 19**
Black Folks	**p. 23**
Cultural Ball	**p. 25**
Do Something	**p. 27**
It Counts	**p. 29**
Freedom	**p. 34**
Black Cool	**p. 36**
Ankh Life	**p. 38**
Little Girl	**p. 40**
Son in Sun	**p. 42**
MDW Netcher Greeting	**p. 47**
Family Greeting	**p. 49**
42 For Life	**p. 51**
Maat Spiral (orange)	**p. 53**
Mississippi	**p. 55**
See Doctor	**p. 57**
UCan	**p. 59**

Cultural Art

Art is this,
Art is that,
Art can throw a kind of ball and be at bat,
It can help a community,
It can help a family,
It can help an individual in more than one way,
It can impact a day,
It can impact a moment, a week, a month to years, centuries and do you not know,
It can be an eye, eyes, hands, a foot, feet, a consciousness and much more,
It can come from a culture, bring a culture and what is the opportunity of cultural healing, not only a feeling, building or reading the top of a ceiling,
This is most definitely art, a start, from the heart, one's part, and it is an opportunity to rest in certainty, relieve stress in ability and be your best clearly through art agility…

Copyrights© 2018   By Vinson Ballard